LOST

WITHOUT ~THE~

RIVER

A Memoir

Barbara Hoffbeck Scoblic

SHE WRITES PRESS

Published 2019
Printed in the United States of America
ISBN: 978-1-63152-531-5
ISBN: 978-1-63152-532-2
Library of Congress Control Number: 2018957239

For information, address:
She Writes Press
1569 Solano Ave #546
Berkeley, CA 94707

Interior design by Tabitha Lahr

She Writes Press is a division of SparkPoint Studio, LLC.

All company and/or product names may be trade names, logos, trademarks, and/or registered trademarks and are the property of their respective owners.

Excerpt from "Found Them Locked Together, Frozen and Other Stories" by W. P. Arndt in *All Hell Broke Loose*, edited by William H. Hull, copyright © 1985 (Edina, MN: Stanton Publication Services). Reprinted with permission of Pauline Conn, Judy Lindberg, and Thunder Bay Press.

Photograph of the Upper Minnesota River Basin by Dennis Skadsen of the Northeast Glacial Lakes Watershed Project. Used with permission of Dennis Skadsen.

Excerpt by Hisham Matar from *The Return: Fathers, Sons and the Land in Between* (New York: Random House, 2016), page 4.

Names and identifying characteristics have been changed to protect the privacy of certain individuals.

LOST WITHOUT THE RIVER

To my sons, Peter and Stephen

And in loving memory of my husband, Joseph M. Scoblic,
and my parents, Myrtle and Roy Hoffbeck

The past is never dead. It's not even past.
—William Faulkner

Contents

PART IV. MOTHER'S TURN

PART V. WE BEGIN TO LEAVE

PART VI. RETURNING AGAIN AND AGAIN

PART VII. FINALE

MAP OF SOUTH DAKOTA

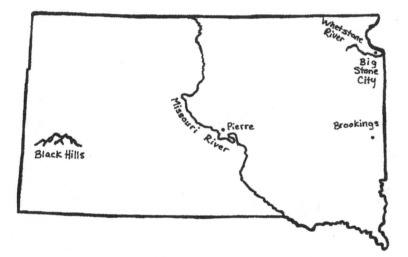

Roy Hoffbeck met Myrtle Chaussee in Brookings, South Dakota. They were married in Pierre, traveled to the Black Hills for their honeymoon, and immediately moved to a farm south of Big Stone City.

MAP OF THE FARM

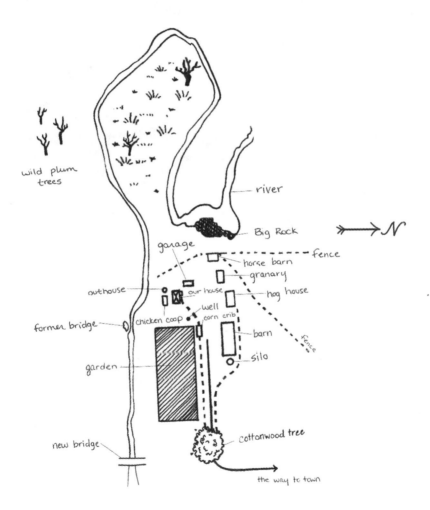

wild plum trees

river

Big Rock

N

garage

fence

horse barn

granary

outhouse

our house

hog house

well

chicken coop

corn crib

former bridge

barn

fence

garden

silo

new bridge

cottonwood tree

the way to town

Northeast South Dakota Glacial Lakes Watershed

The South Dakota portion of the Upper Minnesota River Basin includes three river systems, one of which is the Whetstone River, which flows through our farm. Photo © Dennis Skadsen.

I. PORTRAIT OF A FARM

A FAMILY PHOTOGRAPH

There is no photograph of all of us together.
    There is one of Helen, Patt, John, and Bill, one of those old photographs that make black and gray richer and more real than any modern photograph. The girls are standing. Their hair is in curls, their dresses tied with beautiful, plump bows. The boys are seated in front, wearing white shirts, their feet placed carefully. Helen is looking at the camera cautiously. Patt, not smiling, seems to be daring the camera to tell us who she really is. John and Bill wait obediently for the ordeal to be over.
    There is no photograph of Bob and me with the others. None was ever taken. Someone told me that my grandfather had arranged and paid for the portrait of the four oldest children. Had he grown uninterested by the time Bob and I, numbers six and seven, came along? I wish there were such a photograph of all of us, not just the children, but of the adults as well—one taken, perhaps, when we were all still at home. Before Helen had left for the Twin Cities. Before Patt had begun her frantic attempt to work her way through college in three years, trying to jump-start life.
    What time would I pick for such a photo? What day?

Perhaps my First Communion day—that would have been in late May 1945, when I was about to turn seven. If you ever come to these gently rolling hills in northeastern South Dakota with the farmlands nestled near two clear lakes, decorated with the twisting of the Whetstone River, late May would be the time to make the trip. After a very long, very cold winter, spring erupts in a few days. The aromas of damp earth compete and mingle with the scents of lilac, apple, and peony blossoms. In the evening after a rain, if you breathe deeply, you'll become light-headed, maybe even intoxicated. Such is the sweetness of the night air.

The place for the photograph? The dining room in our farmhouse. Not a large room, and on this day, the day the photograph was *not* taken, almost all table. Bob and I would have stretched the table, splitting it in its middle, so we could add all the extra leaves, lining the little pegs up with the little holes, fitting them together just so, a gigantic jigsaw puzzle. Then we would have placed the protective pads on top, making sure the green felt was down, resting next to the gleaming walnut. When Bob and I finished, Mother would have dressed the table with her largest white damask linen cloth.

My grandfather Bert, the last of my grandparents and the only one I really knew, would be there, speaking with a heavy Danish accent. He died when I was thirteen, and for years I could still hear his voice in my head. When I couldn't hear it anymore, I knew I had truly lost him. My dear Aunt Marian would be there, too. She made the long drive from Pierre for every important family occasion—sometimes with a blizzard hard at the bumper of her trusty 1939 Studebaker.

So, let the photographer pull back with his camera now.

There at the head of the table is my father. To his left are John, the oldest son, then Bill and Bob. Aunt Marian is next. At the other end, opposite my father, is my grandfather. On the other side, at the corner nearest the kitchen, is my mother, looking as though she's ready to spring up, having forgotten something in the refrigerator, perhaps the long relish dish, divided in three parts, with its array of her tempting homemade pickles: sliced chartreuse bread-and-butters with a few celery seeds clinging to them; deep green, sweet chunks; and (even now, as I write this, my mouth waters) her specialty, long, pale green icicles. On my mother's left are Helen and Patt. There on my father's right I sit, still wearing my white dress and white stockings, not worried today about the possibility of my father criticizing my eating habits and table manners. Not today, with company.

My shoes are already off. The only thing Mother ever nagged me about was walking around the house without shoes. She had to work and work to get my cotton stockings clean. But I could not stand wearing shoes in the house. In I'd come, off they'd go. And today, my day, I wanted my shoes off more than ever. I wanted to be white, white, white, white! Veil, dress, stockings, shoes. Not white, white, white, brown. Patt's First Communion shoes were nowhere to be found (there are nine years between us), and Mother said we just could not buy white shoes for only one day or, at the most, one season. So I wore my school shoes. Under the table, no one could see that those shoes were off, my stocking feet curled comfortably around the rungs of my chair.

Okay, this is a good time to take the photograph. I see all of us, suspended. We're waiting for my father. He is about to ask someone to say grace. My brothers, sisters, and I know who he is pleased with on any particular day, at any particular meal, who is in his good graces, so to speak, by who he chooses. Today I'm sure it will be me. Our heads are not yet bowed. We're looking at him, waiting for his word. Here we are, all of us together. Waiting.

His voice is low, soft, actually.

"Barbara," he says. A one-word blessing.

But even my imaginary photo wouldn't be complete. One of us was already missing on that day. The crib was already gone from its place in the corner.

THE FARM AT
THE BOTTOM OF THE HILL

~~~

With a map of the United States, the state lines delineated, I can always point to the exact spot where I grew up. It's a small place, but it's very easy to locate.

Many years after moving away, as I watch CNN's national weather report, my eye automatically tracks to that place on the map. Middle of the United States, one block down from Canada, there's South Dakota. The state is located pretty much in the center of the North American continent—equidistant between the Atlantic and the Pacific, halfway between the North Pole and the equator. At its northeastern corner, there's a small quarter-moon curve cut out. At the bottom of that is Big Stone City. If you turn south on a dirt road at the edge of that little town and follow it for a mile, there's a lone cottonwood tree. Bear right, and you've arrived at our farm.

When I moved to Manhattan, no one seemed to know where South Dakota was. They had a vague sense it was located somewhere west of Ohio and east of California. I was an oddity. "I've never met anyone from South Dakota before" was a new acquaintance's usual response.

Even now. Just the other day, as I was working on this manuscript in my favorite coffee shop, a man stopped and asked what I was working on. When the conversation continued, I shouldn't have been—but was—surprised when he said, "Oh, I've never known anyone from South Dakota."

It was on one of those occasions when I'd again been trying to describe this location to a friend that she said, "It seems to me that you grew up in the middle of nowhere."

After the movie *Dances with Wolves*, filmed for the most part in South Dakota, was released in 1990, my colleagues and friends believed they now knew what my home area was like: endless miles of flat prairie with only an occasional tree. If there were time I'd correct them by describing the geographical differences between the area where the movie was filmed, west of the Missouri River, and where I grew up. The river flows down through the middle of the state, dividing it into two distinct districts, geologically and botanically. When Dakota Territory was deemed too large to govern as one entity, officials made a mistake, I'd explain. They should have split it into East Dakota and West Dakota.

The western edge of the massive glacier that covered the north-central portion of what is now the United States during the Pleistocene Age ended midway through the state. The Missouri River was its western edge, and therefore the landscape to the west was not impacted, but the eastern half was transformed. Glacial activity continued. As the final glacier began receding some twenty thousand years ago, a slow process that would take about ten thousand years to complete, the ice mass ground down boulders into rocks, then into till. It leveled off hills and filled in valleys. Present-day rivers occupy channels originally cut by melting glaciers. After eons, decomposing tall grasses growing in the glacial till changed into rich black topsoil—a step vital for my grandfather and our family.

Early French explorers named the Lateral Moraine, an accumulation of the glacial deposits left behind by that later glacier, Coteau des Prairies (Hills of the Prairie). George Catlin, pioneering author and artist, famed for his portraits of Native Americans, wrote in 1835 that the huge embankment "was the noblest of its kind in the world," and that it offered "the most unbounded and sublime views of—nothing at all—save the blue and boundless ocean of prairies that lie beneath and all around him, vanishing into azure in the distance, without a speck or spot to break their softness."

We simply called it "the hills." On a clear day in Big Stone City, it could be seen as a thin blue line.

Elevation rises slowly, deceptively, from our farm 1,200 feet up to Summit, a small town thirty miles west of us in those hills. The water from melting snow and ice from the eastern escapement of the hills flows into spring-fed streams, which make up the headwaters. All of that water drains into our river, the Whetstone.

That northeast corner of the state where I grew up was left with minimal slope and limited drainage. Masses of ice were left buried in some areas, and when the ice melted, marshes, ponds, and lakes were created, including the two lakes, Traverse and Big Stone, the shapes of which give the state that curved indentation on the map. The surface of Big Stone Lake, 966 feet above sea level, is the lowest point of elevation in South Dakota.

The continental divide runs horizontally between the lakes. Of course, this is just an inflection of the earth's sphere, and, as such, undetectable to the eye. The northern one, Lake Traverse, flows into the Bois de Sioux River, then into the Red River of the North, and eventually on into the Hudson Bay. But drop a piece of wood into the Whetstone River, which feeds into Big Stone Lake and runs just yards (in flood years, only feet) from our house, and, with more luck than our family ever had, it will float down the Minnesota River, then into the Mississippi, and on into the Gulf of Mexico.

Ours was probably the first wood-framed house in the Big Stone City area. It dates to 1873. In that year, there were sod shanties and log cabins in the settlement that was to be our hometown. W. R. Movius, a pioneer who would become the first postmaster and owner of a general supply store in town, laid a foundation, hammered the boards, and raised the roof on the one-room structure.

That building, the origin of our home, became a gathering spot, a place of comfort for pioneer families who met there to pray for endurance, to plan, and to offer solace during difficult times. And those were difficult times. Tragically, that first family lost three young children.

Later, a second building was moved from another location and attached to the existing structure. (The original house would become our dining room, the second, our kitchen.)

Our farm was later owned by the Black family and then by the Sahrs. Those owners remodeled by adding woodwork, a downstairs bedroom, the living room, and a second story. That was the configuration my grandfather purchased in 1913, planning ahead so that his eldest, my father, would be able to walk to the high school in town.

It's easy to understand why Mr. Movius chose that location to build a house for his family. With no bridges, pioneers situated homes in places that were easy to cross. One perfect location was down a gentle decline south of our house where, with no banks, the water of the river widens and flattens out—ideal for fording from the west bank to the east. It's the same place where as children we waded across the river to pick gooseberries.

Several miles upstream, another important building, a post office, was built in a spot with similar terrain. The low stone-and-wood structure, with its cubby holes for mail, still stands.

By the time my newly married parents moved in, the farmhouse consisted of a kitchen, dining and living rooms, two bedrooms on the first floor, and three more on the second. There was no central heating (only a wood- and coal-burning stove in the dining room), no running water, no indoor plumbing. The kitchen had a wood-burning stove with an oven and a tank on the side, which we filled with runoff water. We used that water to clean the house and wash our clothes, thus saving precious well water for drinking. When my mother baked, no additional wood was needed to heat the water. We called the efficient receptacle "the reservoir."

All of the rooms were small; the dining room, the largest, was perhaps twelve by fourteen feet. That room, the living room, and my parents' bedroom downstairs were wallpapered. The kitchen floor was covered with a flat sheet of linoleum; "rugs" of the same material, with floral borders, were laid on the floors of the living and dining rooms.

When my parents moved to the farm after their honeymoon, the white barn dominated the small area between our woods and the hills. It wasn't long, but it was high—thirty-five feet to the top of the roof. So, even though its location tamed strong gusts, it creaked on very windy days.

Regardless of the woodland setting, it was a prairie-style barn of two stories, but with one major difference: it was built into the hill so that wagons could be driven up to a door at the north side, making it easy to load grain, feed for the winter months, into the top level. On the west side, a large drop door on that same second floor allowed half a wagonload of hay, encompassed by a sling and lifted and guided on a rail, to be deposited into that open space in one efficient maneuver. During the first years, the wagons would have been horse-drawn; later, tractors replaced the hardworking animals.

My mother and father had been married for two years when my mother's sisters, Marian and Mabel, who lived in the capital city of Pierre, decided to see this farm their sister described in long letters. When word got out, friends wanted to join them in the adventure. So, on a beautiful weekend in July, six unexpected guests arrived at the farmhouse. There was only my parents' bed and one single bed in the house, so for the first night the city folk slept in the barn, lying on the haymow floor. Blankets helped cushion their backs just a bit. The next night, my mother insisted that they sleep in the small hotel in town.

Although that story was retold over the years—how the first guests of the new couple had slept in the barn—I grew up unaware that the only remarkable feature of our simple house was a legacy from my parents' predecessors, the first settlers. It was a panel of stained glass in the living room window, just to the right of the front door. It was placed above a larger portion of clear glass and was defined in rectangles of golden yellows and pale greens with small triangular inserts of deep blue. I'll never know how those believers came up with enough money to purchase the glass, or where the glass was manufactured, or how it was transported safely. All I have is my imagination: I see the small congregation standing in our living room, heads bowed in a halo of soft color as the morning sun filters through.

The house was painted white, but by the time I was born, that white had become a scarred gray, weathered by years of wind that carried, according to the season, icy snow pellets or bits of dirt that became embedded between and in the boards.

A large unenclosed porch ran the width of the front of the house; its door opened into the living room, adjacent to the stained-glass window. That was the view of the white house that visitors saw when they drove around the bend at the bottom of the hill. Only once do I remember any guest entering or leaving by that entrance. So unusual was the occurrence that the picture is etched in my mind: the late-afternoon sun falling on my mother as she stood by that door, saying goodbye to her cousins who had journeyed from Pierre—a city, after all, a place where they used front doors.

No, everyone—family and guests—used the side entrance that opened into the kitchen. Even traveling salesmen did not hesitate before knocking at the right door. Months would pass, and our front door would be used only once a day.

Year in, year out, my father turned on the radio at ten o'clock each evening to hear the news. Through all those years, after he listened to sonorous voices announcing the collapse of the banks and the economy, Germany marching into his father's homeland, Denmark; the battles of the Pacific, where the neighbor boys fought and died; Korea and Vietnam; the launching of *Sputnik* and man's first flight into space; Kennedy's assassination, he would turn off the radio, open the front door, and step out onto the front porch to check on his most important concern: the weather. Each night, he would look up at our patch of sky, hemmed by the faint outline of hills and trees, and predict what the sky would offer him the next day.

A few miles from us, neighbors' fields stretched out flat. Section lines divided the county into square miles. Originally, these roads were set on the diagonal, but by the time my father was a boy they had been changed to a square grid pattern. Most fields were a quarter of a section and were interrupted only by barbed-wire fences and an occasional swamp, and, in warm months, rivulets of spring water. But our land was broken up by the twists and turns of the river, so that the South Forty—not large, as its name suggests—was our biggest field. Our other fields were carved from small pieces of flatland situated between woods and hilly prairie and the river. Those irregular fields, the river, and the woods were our livelihood and were precious to us, in part because of the variety of botanical offerings they provided.

I find it remarkable that in the late 1880s, a time when, in some parts of the state, mail was still being delivered by stagecoach and wagons, there was a functioning legislature and a court system.

Laws and record keeping were somewhat flexible then. In 1879, Big Stone City was named the county seat by Grant County's board of commissioners. However, in 1881, when the Chicago, Milwaukee & St. Paul Railway was extended west, a new town named Milbank was established. The founder of that new town pledged money to build a courthouse. Which town held the rights?

A county election was held to settle the issue. But Milbank fell just short of the required two-thirds vote and challenged the outcome. The matter was sent to the court.

While the judge was trying to make a determination, Milbank civic leaders decided to take matters into their hands and seize the records from the repository in Big Stone. But these residents had been tipped off—and they were ready. Farmers arrived with pitchforks and guns. Some texts report that Indians (the word everyone used at that time) with powder-and-ball muskets from the nearby Sisseton Wahpeton reservation joined the fray. That story gains some validity when one learns that a portion of Grant County had been under the jurisdiction of the reservation. In addition, the Indians had strong ties to Inkpa

City (which had been one of three small settlements incorporated into Big Stone City).

Together the Big Stone loyalists held off the invaders, all to no avail. Two years later, after more legal complications, the judge, armed only with a pen, declared Milbank the seat of Grant County. It remains so to this day.

When I was young, decades after that raid, old-timers in Big Stone still clung to their resentment. They recognized that they'd lost the economic value that being the site of the county courthouse would have brought them. In 2010, Milbank had 3,300 residents, Big Stone City, 460.

Growing up, I just accepted the fact that Indians had lived not long ago on this land. My father and brothers found several rock war clubs and a grinding stone on our property. My mother used them to outline the small flower garden at the side of the house. We never found any arrowheads, but our neighbors had unearthed several when they plowed their fields.

My father enjoyed telling the story, which he'd heard from contemporaries of that time, of how the Indians used their familiarity and knowledge of our land to their advantage. In those early homesteading years, local settlers were perhaps more frustrated by than fearful of local tribes, who sneaked into farmsteads at night to steal chickens but never harmed a person. However, when a horse, the essence of the farmers' livelihood, went missing, those men contacted the army at Fort Sisseton, some fifty-five miles north. A small cavalry unit, in full regalia, was dispatched. The troops arrived, located the Indians, and pursued them to the top of our hill, where they dismounted. When the soldiers charged down the hill on foot and tried to follow the Indians into the woods, they became entangled in thick, twisting ropes of grapevines. The Indians, safely beyond the vines, taunted the soldiers as they struggled. By the time the soldiers had worked their way free, the Indians had disappeared.

A thousand years earlier, this region had been inhabited by Native Americans who were mound builders. The first Europeans to explore this region were French fur traders, who encountered Dakota Sioux in the seventeenth. The Sioux and the new settlers maintained friendly relations, trading and enduring mutual hardships for decades. A drawing made in 1823 depicts Indian dwellings on the shore of Big Stone Lake in a spot that I recognize.

Anthropologists consider there to be nine tribes of Dakota Sioux. Those who lived on the shores and on the islands of Big Stone Lake belonged to the Sisseton Wahpeton tribe.

Pipestone was—and still is—sacred to Native American tribes. It is a beautiful muted red color. Because the rock is soft, it's ideal for carving and was used to make the bowls of peace pipes—not only by the Sioux but by other tribes as well. (The rock club that my father found, and that I now have on my desk, was chiseled, rather than carved, out of a lower grade of pipestone.) That stone runs in a huge vein near the surface of the land, about ninety miles southeast of our farm. Not just the stone, but all of the land where it's found, is sacred. There was no warring on that ground. Enemy tribes put aside their animosities when they encountered each other there.

We understood why Indians would have chosen this land. In places the woods were still thick with wild vines and bushes, which provided cover. The vines were also a source of grapes. The woods were home to deer, squirrels, raccoons, and a few mountain lions. The fields provided food for prairie chickens, grouse, woodchucks, and gophers. Fish, turtles, and clams were abundant in the river, and mink and beaver lived near and in the banks. A swamp was adjacent to our property. It was home to muskrats, otter, geese, and ducks.

The green of the woods and the meadows attracted song-birds. In the mornings and evenings, notes of mourning doves, blue jays and orioles, robins, swallows, and woodpeckers could be heard. On summer afternoons, the flutelike song of mead-owlarks calmed the nerves, and great horned owls hooted as we closed our eyes at the end of a long day.

In some places where the river ran quickly, the ice never froze hard, even in the depth of winter. The Indians would have had a reliable source of water, and, just as the low hills protected our farm buildings, they would have shielded members of the tribe from high winds.

The last Indian uprising in the United States took place in northeastern Minnesota, two hundred miles from our farm. The Battle of Wounded Knee, some 460 miles west, is often given that sorry appellation, but it was at Leech Lake in 1898, in the Battle of Sugar Point, that the Pillager Band of Chippewa Indians fought government troops. This was only two years before my father was born. He grew up listening to stories about that battle.

When I learned that the conditions that instigated that conflict—the despoliation of Native American land and the destruction of burial grounds—were the same ones that native people are still fighting today, I was shocked and dismayed. And with that realization I wasn't surprised to learn that the probable reason this battle is little known is that seven soldiers were killed, whereas no Native Americans were. Obviously, that news did not make for good publicity at the time and was little noted beyond the immediate area.

The continual presence of those first people on our property seemed real to Bob and me. We often played Indians and tried to move as silently as they did as we walked over twigs and fallen leaves. We never succeeded.

I was in the garden, gathering potatoes, taking my time doing my assigned chore. It was certainly better in the garden than in the house, setting the table for supper. One of my brothers had already dug the plants from the earth. Awkward bunches lay upturned, big and little potatoes held together by their scraggly roots. All I had to do was bang the clumps of roots and knock the potatoes loose. Chunks of hard dirt flew, making miniature dust storms when they landed. Then I picked up the potatoes and tossed them into my pail. *Thud. Thud. Thud.* The pail began to fill up.

There had been several heavy frosts, and the garden looked terrible. All of the bushy green plants had collapsed. They looked like they were very sick. But I loved the smell of dirt and fallen leaves mixed together. When I stopped banging and thudding and listened carefully, I could hear the river gurgle as the water flowed over and gently slipped between rocks.

A horrible cry came from the north, just over the hill. It had to be Indians! I knew it wouldn't help to run from them. Perhaps if I were brave, they'd show me mercy. And so, as the cries came closer, I didn't run, I didn't look up, but kept my head down and my hands clenched tightly around a potato plant. Only when I heard them passing me by, heading toward our house, did I raise my eyes. And there above, in the pale evening sky, I saw the gray V of Canada geese, my noisy warriors, heading south toward their winter feeding grounds.

IN THE BEGINNING

⟍⟍⟋⟍⟋

Whatever was my mother thinking when she married my father? She had to move from Pierre, in central South Dakota, 250 miles east, to a little farm a mile from a little town. She left her family, who, although not wealthy, possessed quality belongings and an innate graciousness. Her trousseau included sterling silver, fine china from France, and a dining table and buffet that, as of 2018, almost one hundred years later, have a place of honor in a granddaughter's home.

She must have realized that living in an isolated farmhouse would be difficult. This is a place where temperatures plunge to thirty-five below. Wind-chill calculations weren't made in those days, but if we factor in high winds, it's easy to understand how winter killed animals—and people—without a flake of snow falling. But, of course, snow did fall and fall and fall each winter.

The house she was about to move into as a bride had neither central heating nor electricity nor plumbing.

Those facts may have flickered through my mother's mind, but she never would have been able to imagine the tragedy that awaited her less than a year away.

My siblings and I know that our parents met at South Dakota State College (now South Dakota State University) in Brookings, a town ninety miles south of Big Stone City. My father was an undergraduate working toward a bachelor's degree while my mother was enrolled in a two-year certificate program to prepare her for work in state government offices. But we were told nothing of how they met nor any specific details of their courtship.

The year after graduating from college, my father, Roy, took a teaching position in the minuscule town of Ree Heights because it was only sixty-some miles from Pierre. That way, the two of them could meet more easily on weekends. My mother, Myrtle, knew he could do much better. He'd graduated at the top of his class. He planned to apply to teach at the Pierre High School in a few years. The salary would be better, and they'd be able to set up their household near Myrtle's sisters and friends, and she'd keep her job at the State House, which she enjoyed. But because Roy refused to give in to the superintendent's demands to raise the grade of an underachieving student, his contract was not renewed. Roy had no chance of finding another teaching position for the fall, and marriage plans were already in place, so his father offered his own farm to the newlyweds, and he and my grandmother moved to a smaller property west of town.

My parents married in 1926. My sister Dorothy was born in 1927, and in the next ten years five more babies joined the family. Those years were concurrent with the Great Depression and the Great Drought. In 1939, I became the seventh.

Photographs, novels, and films have highlighted the desperation of the families caught in the dual crises of depression and drought in the central plains and in Texas, but too little has been told of the hardships of those who lived on the northern plains.

Pick one of those years—say, 1937, the tenth year of the drought—and imagine my father coming home exhausted after another ten-hour day working away from the farm. He would have gotten up at 4:30 a.m. in order to milk the cows before he set off to haul gravel with his faithful horses, Nellie and Babe, at the front of his wagon. He would have returned filthy and exhausted, the cows still needing to be milked, but grateful to have earned three dollars through a WPA project. Myrtle, always in the kitchen at that time of day, would have been waiting for him with her gentle smile and a glass of cold water. She listened and sympathized but didn't tell him about her day, so my father never heard about how exhausted and discouraged she was after caring for Dorothy, ten; Helen, eight; Patt, seven; John, five; and Bob, a new baby. Nor would she have mentioned the terrible pangs of guilt she felt after she'd allowed her parents-in-law to take little Bill.

She'd managed to keep him alive when he had a violent reaction to his smallpox vaccination at six months, and she'd done her best to nurse him during the other times he'd been sick as well. But finally she had to admit to herself—to everyone—that her mother-in-law, who had more time, could do a better job. My father, however, felt relieved, knowing that my mother's workload would be lightened.

Each of those ten years was similar. Very little rain fell, and the winds blew unrelentingly. I grew up on stories of how my family and their neighbors had managed to endure the 1930s, those dreadful years of drought and depression. For ten long years, the lowest proportions of normal precipitation were observed in five states, one of which was South Dakota. These conditions created the legendary dust storm of May 9, 1934, which made both national and international news.

Even so, it was a shock when I learned many years later that dirt from South Dakota had blown eastward, some 1,400 miles, to New York City.

The powerful wind, blowing west to east, originated in Montana. It swooped down through South Dakota and continued full force all the way to the Atlantic seaboard. In New York City, a sunny day turned so dark that the streetlights had to be turned on for five hours.

The *New York Times* said it was the greatest dust storm in US history.

My mother told me how the chickens had gone to roost at noon one day because the air was so filled with dirt it appeared to be night. Could that have been that Wednesday in 1934?

Perhaps not. Perhaps it wasn't the same day; perhaps it was just another one of those endless days when my mother despaired of ever hearing the sound of rain again, of ever having anything free from dust.

Still, these days when I walk the five blocks from my Manhattan apartment to my bit of green, Central Park, I wonder: Is it possible that below the dirt pathway, right beneath my feet, there might be a bit of my childhood farm?

ALWAYS A STRUGGLE

The Dirty Thirties. That was the expression used when I was growing up. But the cosmos doesn't function by man-made units of time. The drought continued into the next decade. In 1940, there was so little rain it was almost impossible to measure.

Some years were worse than others. When I asked my father about that time, he easily recalled the differences: "1931 was a bad year. 1932 was a pretty good year, but there were no prices [meaning that demand was low]. There was a poor crop in 1933. In 1934, there was no crop at all."

It was in that year that he began hauling gravel for the county as part of a WPA project. The supplemental income was essential, because at that time oats brought only six cents a bushel and eggs were sold for a paltry seven cents a dozen. With no hay to feed the cattle, many farmers sold their livestock for fifteen to twenty dollars a head.

One hundred pounds of flour cost only one dollar, but at Christmastime in 1934 my parents didn't even have that dollar. There wouldn't be any gifts, of course. There'd been none for a few years. Nor would there be anything but necessities purchased at the grocery store, but how could there be Christmas without my mother's homemade bread and sweet rolls? And with no pies?

Each time my father did an extra run of hauling gravel, he was paid with a very small check of only a matter of pennies. These hadn't been deposited. In desperation, my mother shuffled through the odds and ends in the junk drawer of our kitchen cabinet, looking for those minimal checks. When she totaled them up, the sum was just enough to buy a bag of flour.

"In 1935," my father goes on, "there was enough rain to lift our spirits, but 1936 was the worst year ever because grasshoppers chomped through all our crops. They ate everything, including laundry that was hung out to dry. Mother resorted to drying it in the house."

The most extreme temperatures in the United States that year were reported in South Dakota: 120 degrees on July 5, 58 degrees below zero on February 17. That summer, the thermometer at our house registered 108 degrees.

My father continues, "In 1937, because of a terrible blizzard in April and rain in May, planting was delayed, so yields were light and spotty. Corn withered because of the high temperatures. And then two of our horses died of sleeping sickness. In 1938, there was no rain to measure. Snow cover helped us a bit in 1939," he said, as he completed the summary.

When at last rain began to fall again, my father was never able to catch up financially. He worked. We all worked. Working defined who we were. He hadn't been able to pay his father the agreed-upon rental payments; my grandfather forgave those. My parents' checking account often had a balance of zero or less. I remember my mother's embarrassment when she'd look at the mail and find an envelope from the bank with a pink slip showing through its window—a flag to the postman that their account was in arrears again.

When the crops were good, the prices would drop. In an attempt to outwit the markets, some years my father raised Hereford cattle or hogs to be fed and fattened, then sold or butchered. For a few years, my siblings cared for rabbits that eventually found their way to our table.

His small herd of Holsteins was a quiet source of pride. The milk was tested periodically by an official of the state dairy association. One of the perks of that man's job: an overnight stay, including an enhanced family supper. A guest, after all, was always given the best. I wonder now who lost his bed to that visitor.

The cream, separated from the milk, provided a meager, month-by-month income, but equally important as the money was the skim milk. That and the eggs from our motley crew of chickens helped feed us kids. We were always hungry.

In the fields, still trusting that nature would produce the right conditions—no late-spring frost, the proper amount of rain at the right time (not too little, not too much, and *oh please God not hail*)—my father rotated the crops. Field corn and sweet corn, soybeans, oats, flax, rye, alfalfa. Year by year, he kept hoping that after the fields had been plowed, raked, planted, weeded, and disced, there would be a decent harvest.

Our river dried up during the Great Drought, the rushing water reduced to a few stagnant holes. But when, after eleven years, rain began to fall again, it revived. When the river had returned to its normal flow, the fish once again began swimming upstream from Big Stone Lake to spawn in water near our house. My brothers speared large carp in the shallows. When I was seven, I tried to manage the long pole with its barbed metal point, but I had neither the coordination nor the strength to hit one of the slithering fish.

The hole off the Big Rock, a large outcrop of smooth granite, became a prime fishing spot. Each year the fish became larger and more plentiful. By 1943, there were so many crappies competing for food that they'd take anything tossed into the water—a few times even baitless hooks. My father caught fifteen crappies while he was calling the cows home (about a crappie a minute). Then my sister Helen and my brother John took turns with the same bamboo pole and continued to catch fish on the same fly, until it finally wore out.

We always complied with the state-imposed limit. Of course, the total limit was large because there were a lot of us, but, as with all wildlife, we caught only what we could eat.

Minutes after we'd taken them from the water, my mother pan-fried our catches in a little butter. She'd stay in the kitchen and continue frying, replenishing the platter, until all of us had our fill of the succulent fish.

Of course, news of this bounty spread fast, and town residents of all ages took advantage of it—the adults driving, children biking or walking, down to our farm. No fancy equipment was needed: kids caught fish using only strings attached to sticks. Our family welcomed them, until, that is, there were so many cars parked in our driveway and yard that my father couldn't maneuver the machinery he needed to continue with the spring planting. He barked at the fishermen from town only once, but word of his displeasure spread quickly. Thereafter they parked to the side, making ribbons of cars along the edges of our driveway.

In an attempt to make our dwelling pleasant and welcoming, John tilled the hard dirt surrounding our house. Together our family sowed grass seed and took care to keep the sprouts well watered. A neighbor gave us some climbing rose saplings. Helen and Patt planted them in front of the porch. The fragrant yellow blossoms attracted pollinators, including bees, which, for a time, built a nascent hive below the roof of our house. Patt planted peonies—white, pink, magenta—at the edge of the garden. Our lilac bushes had survived those dry years as spindly spikes. Now they grew and flowered.

The opening of the peony and lilac blossoms was timely. Large bouquets of those flowers were picked from our yard and placed in buckets to frame the stage of our school auditorium every graduation season. My siblings and I each passed by them as we strode off with our high school diplomas. In the last of those years, it was my turn to take that walk, and, once again, I wasn't concerned about the reception my father would give me as he, the chairman of the school board, handed me, the class valedictorian, a diploma.

After our father gave the go-ahead, Patt and John drove to Ortonville and bought several gallons of white paint. Patt painted the house first and then tackled the barn—a monumental task for one person. I was very ill that summer with a recurring case of strep throat and therefore was mostly unaware of her endeavor. But I've learned that the project went on for weeks and that Patt had to add an extension to the ladder so she could reach the topmost board of the siding.

In a letter to her sister, Mabel, in 1947, my mother reports that Patt got up at 4:30 a.m. to "beat the heat." In that same letter, my mother relates that she got up twice a night to give me antibiotics. My mother and Patt would almost certainly have passed each other in the kitchen. I assume that when they saw one another, when all else was still, each was encouraged as she set about her chores.

A few years later, my father ordered saplings of fruit trees— apple, pear, and apricot—which he planted at the north side of the garden. They joined an old crabapple tree and rhubarb plants; both had survived the long years without rain. The new trees grew and bore fruit, if only intermittently. The pear tree produced glorious clouds of white blossoms and perfume, but the emergent fruit never matured, remaining only as small red berries.

The blossoms were a gift signaling the end of a long winter of toting wood and coal into the house and carrying yesterday's ashes out, the last of shoveling snow to make a path from house to barn, only for another six or eight inches of snow to erase all that effort.

As the rain returned, the natural vegetation revived. With that, birds and wild animals became plentiful again. Pheasants began roosting for the night in trees close to our house. Early one evening my father, leaving the dogs at home, took ten shells and his double-barreled shotgun, and set out. John tagged along. My father bagged eight pheasants in rapid succession after walking only a few hundred yards. Then he spotted another one, sitting on a nearby branch, but he'd already used his last shell. He'd missed only two times.

"We should have brought more shells," John said.

"No," my father replied, "we have enough birds for a few days now."

And then there was our garden. Not large, about a quarter of an acre, it was set by the side of our drive, only a few yards from our house. We saw it each time we stepped out the door; it was a constant reminder that there was always more work to be done. No matter what the weather offered, unlike the vegetables we planted, the weeds thrived. Rain or shine, hail or high winds, our weeds grew.

We could smell the wild onions when they began to bloom, and we tried to keep the cows from grazing in areas of the pastures where the plants grew, but often we didn't succeed, and then we'd be reminded of our failure at mealtimes. The milk in our glasses would taste bitter and unpleasant.

Ever-expanding strawberry plants, with their creeping runners, could not be hoed but had to be weeded by hand. I had to place my feet just so, making sure I didn't step on the plants or the berries. Kneeling was impossible. I had to lean over the entire time. The plants must be in full sun for the fruit to ripen well. It was slow, tedious, hot work. But when I spied one particular weed, purslane, my heart would lift. As that weed grows, it spreads out in a wide circle that eventually resembles a large, misshapen crocheted doily. I'd run my fingers on the ground under the plant's springy tendrils until I located its center. With a firm grip on that main stem and with one hard pull, I'd end up with the entire plant in my hand. Then I'd disentangle it from the strawberry vines and give it a heave-ho off to the side. I'd straighten up, look down, and admire the result. Only black earth showed beneath the dark green strawberry leaves.

For a few years we raised strawberries, not only for our own use, but also to sell. My father and brothers planted them in a low field about a quarter mile from the house. Other family members must have picked berries in that location, but I remember only lonely hours in that field, the sun baking my back. When I went to bed on those nights and closed my eyes, red berry after red berry floated behind my eyelids. Only when my exhausted body took over and I fell asleep did the berries disappear.

Perhaps my mother dreamed of strawberries as well. For after she'd prepared and served supper and the dishes had been washed, small baskets and flat pans heaped with those ripe berries were waiting for her. The berries had to be hulled and washed, then made into jam or canned for sauce before they would spoil, which meant *that* night before she went to bed.

The strawberries and rhubarb, lettuce and cabbage, beans and peas, tomatoes and potatoes from our garden all ended up in my mother's small and modest kitchen. No fancy appliances, no gleaming gadgets. Just the essentials: range, refrigerator, sink, and coffee percolator, always burping gently in the background.

My father and our neighbor Heinie remodeled the kitchen in 1952, when I was in the eighth grade, installing windows on two sides. One of those looked south, to the river a few yards away; the other faced west, designed to catch the sun's last glow as it set behind the hills.

My mother always carefully brushed the little heaps of flour off the breadboard back into the flour bin after finishing a baking project. She knew the price in sweat and prayers of planting and tilling and harvesting even one bushel of wheat. And with that same frugality she always used the last yellow smear of butter in a dish to coat the crisp tops of loaves of bread just taken from the oven. Butter was precious. She was keenly aware of the work it had taken to feed the cows, milk them twice daily, and separate the milk into its two useful parts.

Without saying a word, my mother taught. I observed her as she consistently used every food item, never giving in to the easier route by just throwing something away. When she made an angel food cake that used only egg whites, she made mayonnaise with the remaining yolks. Bread that was no longer fresh was an essential ingredient in her wild plum cobbler. And, of course, she cooked and served all parts of a butchered animal. I remember my revulsion upon seeing a cooked cow's tongue on the cutting board before it was sliced.

But rather than being made stingy by the necessity of frugality, she was consistently generous. If anyone stopped by close to mealtime, my parents invited them to join us at the table. Then I'd notice my mother as she served herself extra small portions. One day, someone arrived just as we were sitting down for our noon meal. Of course, that stranger to me was asked to eat with us. My father told me to get another place setting from the kitchen. The pie had been cut earlier.

"But now I won't get a piece," I complained to my mother.

"Don't worry. You can have mine," she said.

In every season the kitchen was warm with cooking and baking, but in late summer and early autumn it was alive with color as well. Then each surface was crowded with containers holding my mother's works in progress.

In early September, in anticipation of the first killing frost, slightly green tomatoes were lined up on a windowsill to catch the sun that would perfect their color and flavor. In the corner on the floor sat two crocks containing cucumbers on their way to becoming pickles. The contents of one, just sliced and put in brine that morning, were ivory white. The contents of the other crock, which were about to be canned, were now a vibrant green. The aromas of dill and allspice mingled in the air when I passed by them.

An aluminum cake pan on the counter held a heap of red strawberries, their stems still attached. Nearby rested a saucer filled with a pinkish foam, the top fluff skimmed from yesterday's jam making. It would be gone before evening, spread on slices of freshly baked bread. The jars of red jam, with their neat caps of bubbly paraffin, were lined up close by.

A marigold blossom, accidentally broken from its stem, floated in water in a small dish. My mother wasted nothing.

Without our having to expend any energy, the woods and river produced. We had only to gather what was offered there, though that was never easy.

Wild asparagus grew in a few places on the banks of the river. That plant is not a native; rather, it was brought by Europeans who settled in New England in the 1700s. Red berries on the female plants contain black seeds, and some of those seeds and their progeny after escaping, garden by garden, eventually made their way to our farm in South Dakota. As a teenager, Bob plucked the stalks when they first emerged. At our meals those evenings, we savored the taste of spring. The flavors awakened our taste buds after months of eating canned food.

The tiresome gathering of wild berries fell to my sisters and me—and Bob when he was little. Wild raspberries, gooseberries, Juneberries, chokecherries, and ground cherries. They needed to be picked at just the right time. Too early, they'd be sour; too late, they would turn to mush between our fingers. And, of course, the birds were watching those berries just as carefully as we were.

Patt cast herself in the role of taskmaster, and she took to it naturally. Each day she'd prioritize the chores that needed to be accomplished and in crisp no-nonsense sentences tell Bob and me what to do. Almost always what we were told to do was hard work and boring. Complaining wasn't an option. Whom would we complain to? Our mother? We could see that she never stopped working. Our father? Absolutely not. He didn't tolerate laziness or excuses. Two things leavened our discontent: Patt was working hard also, even harder than we were. And her energy and enthusiasm, even if they weren't contagious, made the time go a little faster.

"The gooseberries are big enough now to be picked," Patt called out.

Bob and I knew she was talking to us. After breakfast we gathered the pails—tin cans with shoelaces knotted through holes that had been punched near the top. We put on old, long-sleeved shirts and followed Patt through the pasture gate.

Already it was hot, but as we waded through the shallows of the river the water cooled us, first our ankles; then, slowly, the cold moved up our legs and on up through our bodies. As we walked along, Patt made our endeavor into a contest. Whoever worked the hardest and gathered the most berries would get a handful of chocolate chips the next time she baked cookies.

The bushes were in a clearing, right in the hot sun. We tied the pails to our belt loops so we could use both hands, one to hold up the spiny branches, the other to pick, berry by berry. Mosquitoes found us in no time, and our fingers were soon sore from the thorns that guarded the fruit. We picked all morning, swatting mosquitoes, wiping sweat from our faces with our sleeves, sometimes sucking our fingers when they hurt too much.

When we stopped for dinner at noon, we dumped the contents of our pails into the steel bucket Patt had brought along. All our little berries, some green, a few pink, each with a tiny whisker on top, didn't even fill the bucket halfway.

Patt told us that Mother would use the green ones for sauce, the pink, in a few days when they turned red, for jam. When we got back to the house, Patt surprised Bob and me. We had done a good job, she said. Both of us got a handful of chocolate chips!

Once in a while, the gathering of these fruits wasn't so much a chore as an adventure.

In a good year, the limbs of the wild plum tree in the pasture hung down, heavy with fruit. By mid-August, the fruit was usually ripe. Gathering an old blanket and a large tin tub, my brothers and I set out. We slipped through the barbed-wire fence and headed, single file, for the old tree, led by an erratic corps of grasshopper majorettes and surrounded by the sweet smell of warm clover.

We spread the blanket beneath the tree, and then two of us grabbed a low branch and shook it, sometimes dangling in midair just for fun. The plums came bouncing down in a shower of delight.

After we filled the tub and carried it home, the work began. These plums were only a little bigger than a shooter marble. In early summer, they had been pink with just a hint of orange. Days of sun had reversed the colors. Ripe plums were orange with a blush of pink. They had to be washed, each one pitted. Our eyes were always alert for worms. The fruit was then cooked with sugar and canned in jars that had been painstakingly sterilized.

We often had home-canned fruit for dessert, but this batch was not ready to be eaten, not yet. If you did, the sauce was so sour, even with that added sugar, it would make your cheeks pucker and your eyes tear up.

When winter settled in and the condensation from cooking made mountain peaks of frost on the inside of our kitchen windows, my mother made her wild plum cobbler. She opened a jar of sauce and dumped it into a pan. Then she added sugar and let it simmer on the back of the range. After an hour or so, she tested the sauce to determine if it was ready or if it needed

more sugar. Then, in a large bowl, she put down a layer of one-
or two-day-old bread, followed it with a layer of the plum sauce,
and so on, until the bowl was filled. After that, she placed a heavy
plate on top and set her creation on the back porch to mellow in
the cold. She made wild plum cobbler only in the winter.

When my mother served the dessert, she topped it with rich
cream. The bread, now moist, was sweet but suffused with a slight
tanginess, and lines of delicate pink swirled through its layers.

II. BRIDGE, BARN, AND SILO

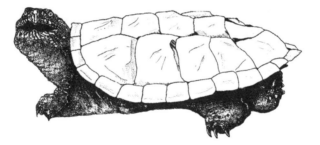

THE BIGGEST

SNAPPER EVER

When Bob was seven and I was five, at an hour when my older brothers and father were already back in the fields after the midday meal and our mother was resting, gathering energy before she resumed her chores, without telling anyone, we slipped away. We went to the barn and found a gunny sack that, after having been used for some mundane chore, had been tossed into a corner. We carried the bag and set out through the gate by the horse barn. As it swung back into place, the pingy sound of metal hitting metal followed us for a while, before gradually fading away.

We headed to the Big Rock. As we set off on our adventure, the midday heat seemed to have called for a recess. Birds rested silently in the cool shelter of the trees. We tried to be just as quiet as we walked along the dirt path. After a few minutes, we could see the top of the rock. As we crept along, we ignored the burning stings on our bare feet as they touched the hot granite.

Bob and I scanned the surface where the rock dropped down to the water. We were in luck! There, taking a siesta, was our prey: a snapping turtle. I followed Bob's silent directions, and in short, slow, synchronized steps, the two of us made our way toward it. Now, each with a hand on a side of the opening of the gunny sack, we advanced until we were right behind it. I pushed my fear down; I was aware that the turtle's strong jaws could snap off a small hand. Then, when Bob motioned, we pounced forward and slung the bag over it. Together we quickly raised the bag, now heavy with its resisting contents. Bob took over. I took a deep breath in and watched as he twisted and tied the top.

"This is the biggest snapper ever!" Bob proclaimed.

With big grins, we each took a side of the bag again. The weight kept shifting unexpectedly from his side to mine as together we lugged our captive.

That day wasn't the first time that Bob and I caught a turtle and carried it to town, but it was the last. Each time when we reached the city limits, we turned onto a driveway that was no more than two ruts with weeds growing in the middle and walked to the second house, where the man who loved turtle soup lived. He never smiled when he came to the door, only turned back and disappeared into the interior. When his huge shape reappeared, he'd open the screen door just enough to drop coins into Bob's waiting hand.

The next summer, our garden produced an abundance of radishes, many more than our family wanted to eat. Together Bob and I pulled the plants, then dissolved the dirt still clinging to the red globes by sloshing them up and down in a pail of water. We made small bundles of radishes, securing them with pieces of string. Again there was the walk to town, farther this time, into the center. We walked to the only grocery store, located on Main Street. We hadn't made any arrangement with the owner, so we just stood by the counter, which was a few inches above my head, until he noticed us. When he did, Bob did the talking. The grocer bought all of the radishes at five cents a bunch. Whether he did this out of the kindness of his heart or because he thought it a profitable deal, I'll never know.

My siblings and I created our own jobs, singly and as a group. John and Bill planted sweet corn. When it was ripe, all of us were in the fields at 4:30 a.m. We worked as a team. John and Bill picked the ears of corn, after expertly determining which ears were ripe by the thickness at the top of the ear. Bob and I counted as they carefully tossed the ears into the bags that we dragged along. My height was a disadvantage—the sharp edges of the leaves left razor-thin cuts on my face—but I was happy to be included and didn't complain. I just kept trudging down the narrow paths between the tall corn plants, which at that hour were still wet with dew.

I would watch my brothers and sisters load the full bags of corn into the truck to be taken to the grocery stores in Big Stone City and Ortonville, another town just across the state line in Minnesota. They were always there when the stores opened, beating out any competition. At the end of the season, John and Bill divvied up the profits, adjusting for the value of each of our labors in some unscientific but fair algorithm. I still remember my share one season: eighteen dollars!

We were alert to new ways to earn money. In late winter I went door-to-door, convincing people, some who I didn't know, that it was time to order Burpee Seeds. The thought of making my own money overrode my shyness. A few weeks later, I'd deliver small boxes containing the varieties my customers had selected. When the ground had thawed, my brothers drove the tractor to town and plowed gardens; some of those gardens would be planted with the seeds I'd sold.

In spring and summer, my brothers seined the river for minnows, which they kept in a large aluminum tank set into the ground at the edge of our lawn. Shade from tall oak trees kept the water cool and the minnows healthy. Fishermen of all ages and both sexes drove down from town to buy bait. And, of course, as spring moved into summer there were berries, water-melon, and cantaloupe to be picked from our fields and sold.

In winter my brothers set lines along the banks of the river, trapping mink, beaver, raccoons, red foxes, and muskrats in the sloughs. At that time, there was a fur trader in every town who would buy the animals, skin them, and transport the pelts to the Twin Cities to sell to a wholesale merchant.

When customers asked for a dozen ears of corn, we always added a thirteenth. When ladling out minnows by the scoop, we added another quarter scoop. And when plowing a garden or snowplowing a driveway, my brothers set the price by the customer's perceived ability to pay.

But when we were accused of not being fair or when we viewed the buyer as unfair, beware! No thirteenth ear ever again to Mr. Kleinschmidt, owner of the grocery store in Ortonville, after he accused Helen of counting a sucker (an undeveloped ear) as one of a dozen. And no generosity shown to Mr. Mounce after our family learned how he treated his wife. To punish her for forgetting to turn off a light, he made her do the laundry by hand for years. So when Mr. Mounce drove down to our farm to purchase minnows, John always ladled out a disproportionate number of bull fish, which weren't appealing even to the hungriest fish.

After Bob and I carried the Biggest Snapper Ever to the man who loved turtle soup and asked him for an additional twenty cents because the turtle was so much bigger than any other he'd bought for sixty cents, and he refused, we turned, left, and carried the turtle back to the top of our hill. We dumped the giant turtle out there, knowing he'd find his way back to the river.

My mother also contributed. She'd stop in the middle of some chore to answer a knock at the door. Cream that had been separated from the twice-a-day milkings of my father's Holsteins was sought out for its richness, perfect for turning into whipped cream or homemade ice cream. She'd fill the glass jar that the purchaser handed her and, with a smile, thank him when he paid her sixty cents.

When Bob was nine and his legs had grown long enough to reach the clutch and brake on the tractor, he deserted me to join the men and older boys in the fields. I continued alone. I accepted a job picking raspberries for my neighbor. These berry bushes thrived because they were in a hollow where high temperatures quickly ripened the fruit. Good for the berries, bad for me. There was no breeze to cool me or blow away the pesky gnats or mosquitoes. Worse than that, the job was boring and lonely. The next summer, I convinced MaryLee, my first friend, to join me. That made the long hours in the sun easier. MaryLee still hasn't forgiven me.

"We were little girls," she said during our last visit. Her voice rose in indignation. "The heat, the prickly spines, the mosquitoes! For a nickel a basket! That wasn't child labor, it was slave labor!"

LIGHTENING THE LOAD

⌇

Throughout the drought and the depression, neighbors met once a month, always in the evening, after the families had finished milking the cows and caring for the livestock. This gathering was called the Farmers' Club. The location of those meetings rotated. The large graniteware coffee boiler and a slatted wooden crate containing sturdy mugs rotated, too. At those meetings the men and women discussed practical matters, of course, but the primary reason they dressed up and drove to the host farm was to socialize with others who were enduring the same travails.

I remember—it may be my first memory—when, on one of those evenings, I crawled under the chair that my mother was sitting on and rested my head on a rag rug as the evening continued. No one could see me. I watched and listened. Songbooks were passed around and page numbers, in no particular order, called out. These were neighbors who didn't look special to me in any way, but when they sang they made music more beautiful than any I'd ever heard. I felt they were singing from their hearts. "Oh, come to the church in the wildwood, oh, come to the church in the dell. No place is so dear to my childhood as the little brown church in the dell. . . ." They'd pause, another song would be named, a scuffle of pages, and they'd begin again.

By this point in the evening, they'd already conducted a business meeting and enjoyed a program. I'm in possession of two notebooks, one with dues of fifty cents for each couple carefully recorded, the other with the scripts for original plays. Sample:

> *"Margaret," moaned Harold, "you promised me you wouldn't buy another dress this season. What made you do it?"*
> *"Dear," said Margaret, "the devil tempted me."*
> *"Why didn't you say, 'Get behind me, Satan'?"*
> *"I did, and then he whispered over my shoulder, 'My dear, it fits you just beautifully in the back.'"*

The characters named in the plays were always real; Harold and Margaret were neighbors of ours whom I remember well.

After the program was finished, the women would excuse themselves and go to the kitchen to fetch more coffee for everyone. The hostess had made the brew by stirring a cracked egg—shell and all—into the boiling mixture to counteract the acidity of the bitter coffee. Each wife had brought a dessert—cookies or a cake, brownies or a jelly roll. The men sampled everything, explaining they didn't want to offend any woman. Of course, all this time, the kids were competing wildly for the sweets.

The songs continued. It would grow late. Then one practical member, remembering the early hour he had to be up the following morning, would begin softly, "I'll take you home again, Kathleen." When that song was completed, another voice would lead with "Good night, Irene, good night, Irene, I'll see you in my dreams."

The men would look at their wives. There'd be a smile and a responding nod. As songbooks were gathered, someone would hum a bit, before starting, "Good night, ladies, we're going to leave you now." All would join in. The empty cups would be carried to the kitchen, the children rounded up, and the thank-yous and goodbyes would begin.

WORKING TOGETHER

C hecking the fields was the best part of the day during the growing season. It was part of my father's routine. In June, as the grains began to ripen, the trips became more frequent. After supper my father would open the kitchen door and, without bothering to step in, call out, "Mother, let's go check on the crops."

In response, my mother usually took off her apron, ran a comb through her hair, and met him at the car. Occasionally, she demurred. "These strawberries will spoil if I don't cook them up tonight."

"Those can wait. The day's light won't. Come," my father told her.

It was clear to me even when I was four that my father wanted her by his side. Without asking for permission, I'd slip into the backseat of the car. My brothers were perhaps fishing, enjoying the last of twilight. I always wanted to see more of what lay beyond our farmstead, and I never let pass an opportunity to escape the confines of my little world.

The route changed according to the time of the season and the year. My father began renting acreage northwest of town once he was a bit more financially secure. Mother and I would stay in the car while he got out and walked into the fields. We were on higher ground here, so, as we waited, we were able to watch the sun slide down toward the horizon. Hills prevented us from doing that on our farm. A breeze would blow through the car windows; my father would climb back in, start the engine, and drive another half mile or so. I was quiet. Crickets chirped from the weeds and grasses near the car, frogs croaked from a nearby slough, and the melodic trill of a meadowlark floated in the air. I'd grow sleepy.

When we arrived back at our house, my father would say, "Okay, out of the car, Barbara. Go get ready for bed."

One evening, his voice didn't rouse me. Instead, when he turned the engine off, I wasn't aware when he pulled the front seat forward, leaned in, and scooped me up. I awoke as he carried me into the house. I kept my eyes closed, relishing this special time in his arms.

My father and the other farmers did their best to predict when the crops were at their peak, but nature never let them forget that she was in charge. In a matter of minutes, high winds could spring up and topple wide swaths of the slender stalks, a condition called lodging, which disrupted the leaf canopy of the stalks, resulting in a lower yield. Or rain might delay the work until the plants and soil dried out.

When, after the Great Drought, the fields had once more begun yielding quantities of oats, rye, flax, and barley, seven neighboring farmers worked communally to harvest the crops. As they moved from farm to farm, men and boys, some as young as ten, worked from early morning until dusk.

Days earlier, a binder had been driven through the fields to cut the stalks of grain and bind them into bundles with twine. Those had been gathered up and placed in small, tepee-like shocks, which allowed for air drying and offered some protection from rain.

The shocks stood scattered throughout the fields haphazardly, like dice cast onto a table. The threshing machine was pulled in. Then the hard work began: the shocks were man-ually tossed into horse-drawn wagons and transported to the threshing machine, which separated grain stalks into kernels and straw, blowing the straw into huge piles. The men were always on a tight schedule. Dad came in one night at ten thirty. They had to move on to another man's fields in the morning. At this point, the farmers paid the owner of the threshing machine a per-bushel rate.

Some years later, new machinery became available. This equipment could make the field work much easier and could lessen the impact of diminished hands as my brothers, one by one, left for college and subsequent summer obligations. Coin-ciding with that upheaval in our family was my father's purchase of a newly available threshing machine. His good friend Heinie supplied his John Deere tractor, and the other farmers fur-nished wagons.

Of course, those crews of men and boys had to eat. The farmers' wives began planning the meals each would serve as soon as the schedule was set. Only then did they know the exact day when feeding the crew of twelve, sometimes as many as sixteen, would be up to them.

To prepare for the Big Day, the previous afternoon my mother would have made a double batch of bread, saving some of the dough to make rolls. The baking—all of her cooking—was done using the wood-burning stove.

The next morning, after serving breakfast to my father and brothers, Mother would make two pies and two spice cakes. While they were baking, she peeled potatoes. I went out to the garden, where I looked for perfectly ripe tomatoes, which I added to the cucumbers and beets I'd already gathered.

Then it was time to make the lunch, which the men would eat in the field at 10:00 a.m. Two kinds of sandwiches made with the freshly baked bread; the cakes, cut into squares; jugs of water; egg coffee, which had been made and carried in the traveling Farmers' Club kettle; and two small jars containing sugar and cream. The kettle's companions, the sturdy Farmers' Club mugs, were carried in their crate.

As soon as the lunch left the kitchen, final preparations for the big meal began. A typical menu: roast beef, potatoes and gravy, boiled beets, sliced tomatoes and cucumbers, cabbage salad, dinner rolls, and—to give the men a choice—both peach and apple pie.

Earlier, my mother had filled a large pan with warm water. The pan, soap, and a flour-sack towel were placed outside the door. The sound of the crew preceded them. Stomping and talking and laughing, they entered and jockeyed for places at the table like teenagers. Mother and I carried in the serving dishes heaped with food. After the men had helped themselves and passed the dishes, for a short time the room was silent as they dug into the meal.

As the satisfied crew, their stomachs now full, walked back through the kitchen, each offered a sincere thank-you. Mother and I filled our plates. We didn't bother to clear the table but sat and ate. Of course the dirty dishes were waiting to be washed and dried, and the second lunch had to be prepared so it could be on its way to the fields by 3:00 p.m.

As they moved from farm to farm, the men worked hard in the fields. They became hot and sweaty. Their reward was eating and enjoying the best of each wife's cooking.

In an unspoken competition, the women always served their specialties. My mother's were her homemade bread and her pies, with their incomparable crust. Heinie's wife, Hattie's, specialty was raised doughnuts, still warm from the kitchen, which she packed in a large aluminum tub and had carried to the field. All these years later, my brothers still talk about those doughnuts.

These were the golden days of threshing: farmers toiling together with enthusiasm and gusto. These families, and other farm families in a ten-or-so-mile radius, were a close-knit group. They didn't always agree, and they didn't share a nationality or a religion. Their bond was the land and the work it demanded.

Later, in 1952, a more distant neighbor purchased a revolutionary machine, a combine. Shocks of grain no longer had to be gathered and lifted up into a wagon. As a tractor pulled the combine through the field, it cut swaths, gathered the plants, and, separating the kernels from the straw, deposited the grain into a bin. A conveyor belt dropped the kernels directly into a truck that trailed behind. The combine saved the men labor and time. The women's workload continued unchanged.

It was in those earlier days when the threshing machine was still being used that the usual routine was interrupted. After we'd returned from church one Sunday (we'd attended the earliest Mass), my father and brothers changed into work clothes, hurriedly ate breakfast, and headed out to the fields.

The ring of our phone on our party line—long, short, long—interrupted the quiet of our house. I was with Mother in the kitchen as she was preparing the big meal of the day. She hurried to the phone at its place on the dining room wall. I heard her say hello, then, after a short while, "I'll be right there."

"Barbara, go change back into your church dress. We're going to the Wachters'."

This made no sense to me, nor did what my mother did next. She removed the special-for-Sunday caramelized sweet rolls from their Pyrex dish and placed the whole circle of them in a brown bag.

Seeing the look on my face she said, "I'll explain as we walk."

We hurried up the driveway. I had to do an extra hop every few steps to keep up with her.

"Something very sad has happened. Mr. Wachter died this morning."

I had never thought a mother or father could die.

We took the shortcut by leaving the dirt road and crossing an untilled hill. The white house sat in the open. The yard, which was smaller than ours, had only a few flowers near the door. I knew this place. It was all familiar to me. Delores, who was a year older, and I sometimes played together.

Mrs. Wachter came to the door. She had on the apron I liked, the one with the yellow sunflowers, but nothing else was familiar. Her face was swollen, her hair uncombed. She didn't give me a hug. She didn't even look at me.

"What am I going to do?" she wailed. She fell into my mother's arms.

As she held Mrs. Wachter, Mother looked down at me, "Go up and talk to Delores."

I climbed the narrow stairs. The second floor was small, the ceiling indented in two places by the shape of the roof. Delores and I had spent long afternoons here, hanging up sheets and blankets, turning the space into a multiroom mansion. In one of those rooms on a rainy afternoon, Delores and I counted her comic books. This had been special. I knew if my family did have extra money to spend, we would never use it to buy comic books.

I stopped as I reached the top step. Dolls and toys were tossed about. The comic books were torn and spread all over the floor. I started to ask, "Who?" But then, with a terrible feeling in my stomach, I realized it was Delores who had wrecked her own treasures. Delores didn't look at me. She stayed seated on the floor. I didn't know what to do. The two of us sat there without saying a word until my mother called, telling me it was time to go home.

Monday morning, the neighbors conferred. Early the next day, shortly after sunrise, a procession, with the John Deere tractor in the lead, traveled to the top of the hill, where they harvested the fields of the grieving widow.

AN EYE ON THE RIVER

⌐⌐

"**B**arbara. Pour some more coffee for Heinie."
Other neighbors were Mr. This and Mrs. That, but
Heinie was always just Heinie. And his wife was always just Hattie.

My mother told me they were my godparents. I felt really
good about that, until my brothers informed me that this was
because by the time I came along—that's the way they said it,
"by the time you came along," as though I were found wandering
down our driveway one summer afternoon—my parents had
run out of Catholic relatives and friends to serve as godparents.

"And please take him an ashtray. Not that it will do any
good." Mother dropped her voice to a whisper when she said
the last.

Heinie had a habit of smoking without knocking the ash off
his cigarette, without even taking it out of his mouth between
puffs. When he smoked, Heinie removed the cigarette only
once, right after lighting it, when he took a breath in. Ever after,
it stayed at the left corner of his mouth, secured by a little curl
of his lip.

I'd watch, trying not to stare, as Heinie continued to talk
and the ash continued to grow. It grew longer, wound up a little,

thinned out, began to crack, and then, at last, dropped on Heinie's pants leg. Without pausing, he'd try to pick up the ash, succeeding only partially, aim what he'd managed to pick up at an ashtray, if one were nearby, or, more often, place the ashes in the cuff of his work pants, never pausing as he continued his story.

"Damn!" That was as profane as Heinie or my father ever got in my mother's presence.

"All those years our land was blowing away without rain, all those years of trying to keep families and livestock alive without water. Now we have that beautiful snow cover ready to soak in, and it turns so warm, so fast, the earth's still frozen and that water's running right down into that river of yours, adding to all that melting ice."

He took the cigarette butt, and, even though I'd put the ashtray right in front of him, out of habit he put it into his pants cuff, some part of him unable to let all those years of drought go, years when the end of a cigarette tossed carelessly would ignite tinder-dry grasses and weeds and bring disaster.

"Thanks for the coffee, Myrtle. And those sweet rolls. Good as ever," he said, as he passed through the kitchen.

He paused at the door with his hand on the knob.

"And, Roy, if it stays this warm, I'd keep an eye on that river of yours."

THE RIVER

⟶

The river was a part of our family, with its own personality and moods. Sustaining, playful, violent. Ever-changing.

In summer, in a few places where the river narrowed, I could walk across it on large stones without getting my feet wet. Just a game. I was always barefoot in summer. There was one pool off the Big Rock that stayed deep, dark, and cool. Perfect for swimming. If I husked the sweet corn just picked from our field quickly enough, there might be time for me to join my brothers for a short dip while my mother finished the noon meal. Swimming spiked our appetites. Even so, when our mother called, "Dinner's ready," we took a few more shallow dives and lazy paddles around the pool before we grabbed towels from the rock and raced to the house.

In early winter, the river froze in a few places. Our parents cautioned us about the thin ice, and I looked at the river but never tried to cross to the other side. Instead I walked along the river's edge, watching where the water bubbled up through holes in milky-colored ice as it moved quickly over the shallows. As I walked through a pristine new layer of snow on the bank, I kept my eyes open for the trails of rabbits, squirrels, and other small wild animals. Their tracks were as precise as cookies, stamped into dough with cutters and lined up on a baking sheet waiting to be placed in the oven.

After several days of subzero weather, the river was ready for skating. Bob and I kept to the main pool, where the ice was thick, but occasionally our older brothers guided us safely around dangerous patches of thin ice as we skated farther from the house.

The familiar banks of summer were gone. Brown stalks stood where there had been impenetrable green weeds and bushes. Animal burrows that had been hidden could now be seen. Colors were muted, and the cold air sent our voices far away into the distance.

On a few enchanted nights, my brothers and I skated downriver by moonlight. In the cold air, our breath rose around us in ever-changing clouds. The sky was an overturned bowl above our heads. The stars crowded each other, the Milky Way a magnificent, sparkling sweep across the curve of the universe. The moon hung large and lemon pale. We were alone in the world. The only sounds were the rhythmic scraping of our blades, our shouts, and our laughter.

Even at its most vulnerable, the river provided for our lives. When it dried up during the Great Drought, only a few stagnant pools remained. That water was reserved for the cows. Because there was no hay, Russian thistle, commonly called tumbleweed, substituted for their feed. The cows' milk was, of course, separated into cream and skim milk. The cream was sold for pennies. The skim milk was mixed with bran and the tumbleweed and fed not only to the cows but to the other farm animals as well.

Turtles, without any place to hide, were easy to catch, and so turtle soup supplemented our diet.

Heinie supported his family on the damaged goods of our dried-up river. During that desperate time, he shoveled mounds of clams and other shellfish from the dry riverbed. After shucking and drying them, he poured them into gunny sacks. Wagons full of these shells were then transported by train to Minnesota and Iowa, where they were made into buttons. He also caught live turtles and placed them into hogshead barrels, which were then shipped by way of Chicago to New York City, where turtle meat was considered a delicacy. Our turtles were served in the finest restaurants in Manhattan, at times perhaps enjoyed by women wearing dresses adorned with buttons made from shells salvaged from our river.

I was too young to be aware of this activity, but a few years later, when I heard neighbors talking about the turtles and the shells, I yearned to go to those faraway places, see the women in their fine clothes.

The river's channel where it abutted our property was changed in the late 19th century in order to supply water to a grinding mill. In 1939 the Highway Department determined that increased traffic on Highway 12 required a longer, more stable bridge at that location. They tore down the old bridge and dug a new channel at a different, and, in their reasoning, more efficient, angle, and placed the new bridge on a portion of our land. This project rerouted the force of the river so that its water bore directly toward our farmstead. The banks of the Whetstone are a huge natural funnel. To protect people and property, a small earthen dam had been constructed years before at Lake Farley, twelve miles upriver.

For our family, spring often brought worry and fear. In years when the temperature rose quickly as winter lessened its grip, the icy earth was a barrier that prevented the runoff from soaking in. The riverbanks couldn't hold the runoff. Then all of us watched the river, not with a view to its beauty, but with apprehension. As the ice on the river melted, huge blocks of it—some larger than our dining room—broke free, drifted as far as a curve, got caught in the trees along the side, and dammed the river. The water rose and came closer and closer to the house. At night I'd fall asleep listening to the whacks of those ice cakes hitting each other, and the moaning and grinding of trees as the ice rubbed against their trunks and low-hanging branches.

There were two major floods during my childhood. From a safe distance of decades, they've acquired affectionate names: the Year the Chicken Coop Floated Down the River and the Year the Bridge Went Out.

The force of those two floods changed the terrain of our farm. They ripped away gentle curves and toppled large trees, leaving new channels and sandbars in their wake. When the waters receded, they left behind a mess of broken limbs, downed trees, and soil filled with stones and debris.

The one constant was our Big Rock, the solitary, irregularly shaped outcropping of granite just north of the horse barn. Over centuries, rushing water had polished it smooth. The large stone seemed somewhat ominous because of a vertical hole that ran straight down through it, the result of a test boring done years earlier. The sample of granite had been determined to be of low grade, and so the stone, with its signature hole, remained, forever marked as inferior. All of us, children and adults, used the rock as a point of reference. "Twenty yards north of the Big Rock," we'd say, or, "Downstream from the Big Rock about a quarter of a mile."

In spring we sat and fished from it. In summer Bob and I scanned it for turtles, and we all used it as a diving board. In winter we sat on its jutting point to adjust the laces of our skates.

The rock was not visible from the house or our yard, and, even into adulthood, when I needed solitude I'd head to it. But during all the years I lived there I was unaware of its most important function: the Big Rock protected us during floods by diverting the raging water and the large blocks of ice away from our house.

By the time the small buildings closest to the swollen river were about to be swept away that day in 1943, my father realized that there was no time to drive to town and buy or borrow additional rope. The water raged only feet from our house, and the mill pond on the other side of our hill had overflowed. Water was now beginning to encroach on the road to town.

My father had one long piece of rope and a major decision to be made quickly: save the outhouse or save the chicken coop. Reality prevailed. He secured our outhouse to the large basswood tree near the south porch. The excitable hens were taken to the barn, while the baby chicks were brought into the house. Patt laid newspapers in the hallway at the top of the stairs, and Bob and I fenced in the little chicks by stacking old copies of the *Saturday Evening Post*.

My age shielded me during that day of fear and turmoil. My memory is one of playing with fluffy little bodies of yellow.

Bob still remembers the stern tone of my father's voice: "Take Barbara and go to Grandpa and Grandma's. Go straight there! Remember to call as soon as you get inside." My father began to stride away, but he turned back and said, "And don't go near the water!"

And so Bob, age five, took the hand of his three-year-old sister, and, leaving the rising water and the rising panic, the two of us headed up the hill and walked the twisting dirt road, a mile and a half to the peace and quiet of our grandparents' home.

A short time later, the chicken coop was seen bobbing down the river.

When Bob and I returned to the farm after a few days, the water once again flowed gently. Everyone was working, and we were expected to work also.

"Take these pails," one of our siblings told us. "There are fish trapped below the house. Go catch some of them."

Dutifully, we set out. The field was littered not only with debris and pools of water but also with giant, dirty chunks of ice. We really did try to catch the fish, but they always slithered away. And adventure, in the guise of the ice cakes, beckoned. Bob somehow managed to scale one that was perhaps six feet high. He then leaned way over and pulled me up. When we stood on that ice, I got a powerful new perspective. I was on the top of the world! Of course, we didn't ponder this for long. This was a great chunk of slippery ice! Bob took a short run and then slid, stopping just before the edge. I began to copy him and started to take a run, when there was a shout.

"Get down from there!" It was Patt.

"Why?" we asked in unison.

"You could slip and break your neck! That's why!"

Obediently we slid down, picked up our buckets, and again set off to try to catch the trapped fish.

A large old cottonwood tree stood as a sentinel at the end of our driveway. It was a reminder to slow down before you turned left and began to drive up the hill on the narrow road. But if instead you turned right, about seventy-five yards down a steep decline there was a beautiful white bridge.

If you paused at the base of that tree and swiveled your head just a bit, you would see our traditional white barn with its companion, a white silo. All three—the barn, the silo, the bridge—were stately representatives of utility, necessary for the survival of our farm.

The white bridge of my childhood was the second that had been built on our property. The first had been situated very close to our house, down a steep cliff at the end of our yard. It collapsed before my siblings and I were born, but concrete fragments of its abutments remained on both sides of a pool that had been scoured out over centuries by fast-running water forced through a narrow channel.

The white bridge was eighty-four feet across, constructed some twelve feet above the water, and composed of four sections. On the sides, plank braces crisscrossed the pilings, creating elongated x's, ideal spots for me to rest my shoulders and head comfortably while I peered over the edge. I watched and waited. Minnows swarmed, a large fish occasionally broke the surface, and bugs did the impossible and walked, Christlike, on top of the water. At the edge, frogs broke the quiet by making splashes much larger than their little bodies. At times I'd spot a giant snapping turtle swimming slowly near the bottom or a group of mud turtles sunning at the water's edge.

Eighty inches of snow on the ground. The earth still frozen solid. It became unseasonably warm in just a few days. The river was on all of our minds in March 1952. We began to keep watch on the rising water.

In the morning, Bill went to town to do an errand but returned almost immediately.

"They say the dam is going to give way!" he yelled before he was even out of the car. "We have to start sandbagging."

Helen was in Minneapolis, Patt and John away at college. My father hurriedly began to gather gunny sacks from the barn. Bill and Bob hitched a trailer to the tractor and drove across the bridge to our small gravel pit. The three worked together to sandbag the cellar entrance and the foundation of the house nearest to the river.

Mother and I began to carry the silver, china, and crystal stemware to the upstairs hallway, the same place where Bob and I had played with baby chicks a few years earlier.

While we were doing those chores, the rushing water was at work, also. We hurried about, unaware that its force had loosened a huge ice cake from its hole at the site of the original bridge. The torrents carried that chunk of ice downstream as far as our bridge, where it became wedged.

Late in the afternoon, after my mother and I had carried everything that we could upstairs, I walked out of the house and into the yard. Outside, I could not ignore the cacophony of sounds as branches snapped, ice cakes hit trees, and water roared when it was forced through the narrow opening below the edge of the lawn. The huge ice cake that had worked its way under the bridge was forced violently upward by the rushing water. Then there was an explosion. A terrifying sound bounced off the low hills and returned, hitting my eardrums in waves. The bridge splintered into pieces.

Rocks and tangled branches caught a portion of the bridge. Bill and my father managed to secure it to a tree. Later, my family made good use of its lumber.

Days after the flood, town residents found pieces of our bridge at the edges of Big Stone Lake, eight miles downstream. The wood was salvaged and reused, perhaps to fix a garden fence, mend a door, build a doghouse. Our bridge was no more.

THE NEXT MORNING

he morning after the flood, everyone was grumbling. The water had gone down, and with it our fear, but there was a deadness in our voices and everyone moved more slowly.

The work to be done weighed all of us down. Two miles of fence in the South Field to be fixed; the corner posts realigned, other posts replaced; wire pulled from piles of debris, untangled, and restrung; forty gunny sacks of gravel that were used to sandbag our house to be emptied and piled for future use, at least three fallen trees in the feedlot to be cut and hauled off; and whole, long, low hills of misplaced earth and sand to be leveled out in the fields where they now rested.

And, of course, there was the house. The first floor, where muddy feet tracked back and forth, to be scrubbed; at least eight loads of laundry to be done, each pair of pants dense with dried mud, the socks turned brown; and the sheets, dreary with dirt tossed off from bodies too tired to wash up, to be soaked and bleached before being laundered.

Even though it was only midmorning, my mother moved slowly as she picked up the coffeepot and went to the table to pour coffee for my father. I didn't need to be told to pour milk and put out cookies for my brothers. It seemed as though they had just left the house, but now here they were, back again, with their big bodies and loud voices. I liked it when my mother and I were in the house without them, listening to the radio as we worked together.

Bill began, "I'll go to town and get wire and posts. If we start right after dinner, we should be able to get ten or so in the higher ground before dark."

I listened. Sometimes it seemed as if Bill really liked to work.

"Okay," my father said. "I'll take Bob out to the West Field, see if we can level some of that dirt before it dries out too hard. I wonder what damn weeds the river has given us this year."

I knew the reason Father said "damn," not "dang," was that he hated weeds. He hated them the way some folks hated sin.

Russian thistle, Canadian thistle, sow thistle, bull thistle. Dandelions and false dandelions. Slowpoke and creeping Jenny. Horseweed and lamb's-quarter. Sandburs, cockleburs, poison ivy, and purslane. Milkweed, wild hemp, wild oats, wild mustard. And, the most hated of all, leafy spurge.

Each time my father said "leafy spurge" he almost spat the "s." His tone reminded me of the time when a visiting priest gave a sermon on the sixth commandment, the one that said, "Thou shall not commit adultery."

Weeds. Weeds producing seeds. Seeds with silk wings that floated on breezes. Seeds, rough and barbed, that rode as passengers on the hides of my father's cows, in the dog's fur, and on the family's clothes. Blackbirds, crows, hawks, even robins, meadowlarks, and orioles, carried the seeds in their guts, carried them long distances, from pastures in other townships, other counties, other states.

All came to rest in my father's fields. And this year the floodwaters had added even more. The next summer, and summers years from then, my father would still be waging war against the weeds that year's flood brought—persistent, unwelcome memorials to our fear, hard work, and survival.

SAME CHORE
DAY AFTER DAY

⌐

As a small child, I longed to have my mother's undivided
attention, and each day there was one special time when
I had her all to myself.

Every day, even Sundays, even Easter and Christmas, my
mother had her chore that she had to do. John or Bill brought
in the water, but from there on, the chore was hers.

She dipped the hot water out of the box on the side of the
stove in the kitchen, poured it into a large tin kettle with a lid,
and carried it to the barn.

I went with her. It was the only time I had her all to myself.
In the house, she was always busy, busy, busy, and even at the
quietest times of day, Dorothy was always there.

My mother called, "Barbara, I'm going to the barn."

I loved setting out, just the two of us going on a journey,
even though the barn was only a little way off. I skipped along
by her side. When we reached the barn, she opened the door and
I held it with my whole body as she walked through.

My mother's chore was to wash all the shiny, silvery parts
of the separator. That machine divided the milk into two—the

milk we drank and the cream that on some days Mother turned into fluffy whipped cream. She told me the separator must be kept absolutely, perfectly clean, or when we sold our cream in town, it might turn sour.

I called, "Kitty, kitty, kitty," slowly the first time, then faster and faster. The cats twined around my legs, showing how much they liked me. They were afraid of my father. Once, when he was milking the cows, Stony couldn't wait for his supper and kept running under Father's feet. Before I had time to call him back to me, my father kicked him. Hard. Up and up Stony flew, almost to the top of the barn, it seemed. Then he started falling down. When he landed, *thur-ump*, I ran to him. I was afraid Stony was broken, maybe dead, but he only staggered a bit as I rushed to pick him up.

I brought the old, bumpy tin pan to Mother, and she filled it with milk. The cats rubbed against my legs so that I almost couldn't walk, but I made them wait until I reached the straw next to the feed box. When I put the pan down, I watched their happy tails as they drank. When they finished, all of us snuggled in the spiky straw.

One time when my mother called for me, I didn't immediately join her. It was on a summer day, a few weeks before my fourth birthday.

My sister Dorothy was in her crib in my parents' bedroom. The late afternoon's light shone softly on that corner, and the window was open just enough that the lace curtains moved gently with the breeze. I was jumping on the bed, carelessly defying the rules. Each time I jumped, Dorothy wiggled her legs. I'd not seen her respond that way before; usually she just lay there quietly. My ability to entertain her felt important. Nobody else had done that. The only time anyone noticed me was when I did something wrong. I jumped again, higher, and then higher still, as Dorothy continued to kick.

"Barbara! I'm going now."

I've tried hard to remember: Did I go with my mother and leave Dorothy disappointed and deflated? Or did I stay and keep jumping, the two of us laughing, until I ran out of breath?

A little more than a year after that, I did do the right thing. The winter sun hit the frost that had collected on the inside of the windowpanes and set off tiny explosions of diamonds. Above the floor where the light streamed in, bits of dust dangled and danced. I felt virtuous. I hesitated and then stepped into the light.

I carefully carried the dish with Dorothy's meal. For once, I was happy that I was too young to be in school with my brothers and sisters. I was the only one my mother could ask to help her. She had sprained her ankle the day before and was in bed. She had gone down on the ice with a cry of pain. My mother never shouted, never even talked loudly, so the shock of that sound was worse than the sight of her on the ground. She hadn't asked to be taken to a doctor but instead took a chair from the dining room and, resting her knee on its seat, hobbled around the house.

The dust bits disappeared as the light shifted. I walked slowly into the bedroom. The dish was not cut glass, shiny bright, like the special dishes my brothers were allowed to carry on the altar at church, but I carried it just as carefully as they did, with both hands directly in front of me. The spoon rested upon the darkening fruit.

I'd followed my mother's instructions exactly, mashing and mashing the banana so that there wouldn't be any chunks that Dorothy might choke on. The banana had slipped away again and again, but I'd patiently pursued it up and down the sides of the dish.

As I entered the small bedroom, I was all business. I didn't even glance toward my mother, lying on the bed, for her smile of approval, but went right to the crib and began to feed my seventeen-year-old sister.

ALWAYS THERE

⟿

As a young child assumes her parents will always be there for her, my siblings and I took for granted that the barn, silo, and bridge would always be there, serving the needs of our family. But structures that we take for granted can also pose unexpected dangers. By the time Bob and I began to roam our farm, discovering nature's surprises, the silo had already been the location of a tragedy narrowly averted. And, not that many years later, the barn also could have been the site of a disaster.

I never really believed Patt when she told me about the silo incident. After all, she was the sister who, in her early teens, had sworn she'd seen a whale in our river. But in 2015, John told me about the incident. The solemnity with which he told about that day wiped away all my doubts.

John tells his story:

On an autumn day when I was four and Patt was six, he began, we were bored and Patt thought she had a great idea. She said, "Let's go into the silo."

Patt went first. She climbed up the steps on the outside of the silo, opened a small door, and dropped down inside. I followed her and jumped through the open door. The silage was warm and squishy under our bare feet, and we began to dance around.

After we'd danced for a time, we sat down for a bit, when Patt said, "I feel dizzy. Let's get out of here."

But when we tried to leave, we found that neither of us could reach the lowest sill of the opened door.

"John! Help me get up higher."

I pushed hard on the soles of her feet, and she stretched her arms up high. She was just able to reach the lowest place to grab and, with that, able to open another door. The deadly gas produced by the fermenting silage flowed out and we were able to breathe good air again. We had gotten out just before it overcame us. A few minutes more, and we would have died.

When I think of that, the real miracle of my life, I don't thank God so much for my or Patt's benefit, but I think of our mother, and I thank Him with her in mind. After Dorothy, she never would have survived the loss of two healthy children.

As John finishes the story, he reaches for his handkerchief and brushes tears from his eyes.

A SUMMER AFTERNOON

~

"Barbara. Barbara! Where are you?"
My name seemed to come from far away, disrupting my four-year-old dreams. It had been so hot that afternoon, and everyone else had been busy, so I'd slipped off to the secret hideout. Only my brother Bob and I knew about it. No one could find us. Even we had to stoop to get under the tangle of wild grapevines. There, where the exposed roots of an old oak tree made steps, it was cool and shadowy. Bob and I had lined up rocks that we'd collected from the low spot in the river. I'd been trying to decide which was the prettiest, when I'd fallen asleep.

"Barbara! Dad says to hurry. He thinks a tornado is close by."
Bob grabbed my hand and pulled me up.

"What's a tornado?"

"It's a terrible, horrible, giant windstorm."

His voice grew louder with each word.

We ran across the yard. When we reached the kitchen door, our mother was waiting with a flashlight and a pile of blankets in her arms.

"Bob, take this light, and the two of you go open the cellar door."

The air was still, but the leaves on the old basswood tree moved gently. Working together, Bob and I swung each side of the double-hinged door up. Then we descended a few rough steps to a small landing. There, we opened another door.

The light Bob carried struck the jars, rows and rows of canned vegetables and fruit. Jars of jellies and jams sat on the shelves like enormous jewels, red, purple, orange.

In the back, beyond the jars, there was a large hole hollowed out of the dirt wall. The previous fall, Bob and I had carried carrots, beets, and potatoes from the garden to the cellar. I'd stayed outside the black hole and handed the vegetables to Bob so he could place them in the back. I didn't have the courage to go any farther.

On the summer afternoon of the storm, I told Bob I was scared.

"I'm not," he told me. "This is fun!"

Mother came down then. She still held the blankets to her chest.

"Bob. Shine the light to the door."

My father started down the stairs. He couldn't see over the burden in his arms. I watched as he carefully checked each step before putting his weight down. The wavering light shone on my father and Dorothy. I'd never seen her out of the crib, even though she was much older than I—even older than my big sister, Helen. He supported her head, but her arms flopped loosely.

"Make a bed with those blankets in that corner, Mother."

He dropped to his knees, and together they laid Dorothy on the blankets. Mother covered her with another blanket. She then sat down and nestled Dorothy's head in her lap. I huddled close by.

The tornado skipped over the five of us sheltering in the cellar that June day in 1944.

My father couldn't have seen the tornado. The small hills that ringed our farmstead didn't allow for a wide view of the sky, but he had a keen sense of the atmosphere, which he'd honed through years and years of practice. His nose could detect subtle changes in the weather. And that afternoon he'd smelled impending danger.

That same afternoon, my brother John, who was twelve, was cultivating corn in the open fields northwest of town. He was alone, concentrating on keeping the teeth of the disc in the dirt path between the rows. The machine was uprooting weeds, and if John veered just a little off course, he'd damage the young corn plants.

The noise of the tractor's engine blotted out any other sounds, but John felt a shift in the wind and looked up. A large funnel was racing across the sky, directly toward him. There was nowhere to seek shelter, only a small, open-sided corncrib off to the side of the field. The building offered no shelter. Corncribs are designed to maximize air flow; their walls are composed as much of air as of boards. He cut the tractor's engine, hopped down, and ran toward it. Below the crib, a slot in the earth had been dug out, each side secured by two-by-four planks. The construction allowed enough space for a truck box to be tilted up to dump a load of corn. John didn't look back, just ran as fast as he could. He managed to shimmy into that shallow slot, where he lay facedown and prayed.

The tornado passed over him.

When writing this story, I called John in Indiana to query him about details of that long-ago afternoon. As he was describing his hiding place, the tone of his voice shifted from animated storytelling to gravely philosophical.

I was so surprised by the timing of what he said next that I stopped taking notes and had to ask him to repeat himself.

"What was that, John?"

"Tornadoes are like love," he said, "When you see it, you don't have to ask if it's real."

FALLING DOWN

—⌐

H oly Saturday, the day before Easter 1945, was cold and
dreary, no sign of spring. But Lent, with all of its restrictions, was almost over. Aunt Marian had arrived a few days
earlier, bringing an array of special foods and abundant love.
And! I had a new coat to wear to church on Easter morning. It
was a beautiful spring-sky blue. Periodically I'd run upstairs,
go to the small bedroom my sisters shared, and open the box to
make sure it was still there.

Because no spring field work was yet possible, John, Bill,
and Bob decided to play basketball in the hayloft. Hay was piled
high along the east end of the large, open space. When we
moved about up there, crunching the scattered remnants of the
dried alfalfa with our feet, a sweet, spicy smell was released—a
fragrant memento from last summer. On the north side, there
was an opening in the floor so that hay could be pitched down
to the cows. Earlier, my brothers had nailed a metal hoop to a
stud on the west wall at approximately regulation height.

Mother and Aunt Marian were in the kitchen. They were
talking and laughing as they made bread and rolls for the following day. Feeling left out, I put on my old coat and went to the

barn. I heard the thump of the ball and my brothers shouting above me. I climbed up the wooden rungs and asked if I could join them. They were in a generous mood. I couldn't play, they told me, but if I stood near the wall, they'd let me retrieve the ball when it went out of bounds.

I waited. Soon a ball came bouncing off to the side. I ran for it, threw it to my brothers, stepped back, and fell down. Ten feet down! I landed on the concrete feeding trough below. I was brought back to consciousness by rhythmical tugs on my face. A concerned cow was licking me with her rough, wet tongue.

My brothers had run to the house to get my father. I was crying when he arrived. He picked me up in his arms. I could feel his thumping heart as he held me and carried me back to the house. My mother and Aunt Marian were waiting at the door. Their faces were scrunched with worry. Marian asked me questions and put me to bed. After she talked to my parents, she told me I must stay in bed for two days. I wouldn't be going to church Easter morning!

The blue coat? It remained in the box on that special day. But after that I wore it every chance I got. Until it became too small. Then it was given away. I do have a lasting reminder of that Easter, however. I carry it with me.

In 2008, X-rays were taken of my cervical spine. In answering questions about my medical history, I told the doctor what happened on that distant Holy Saturday.

"Yes, I can see that. The damage of that fall is visible right here," she said, as she pointed to a spot on my upper spine. "You were very lucky."

"What do you mean?" I asked her.

The doctor paused and then replied, "A very slight shift in that location would have left you paralyzed."

III. FAITH AND PUNISHMENT

"Never praise a child. He'll just wind up being conceited."
—Roy Hoffbeck

OPERA IN THE KITCHEN

———

O pera reigned in our kitchen on Saturday afternoons. When my father was out of the house, working in the fields or perhaps shoveling snow, there was freedom—freedom to shut down the rapid-fire tallies of grain and livestock futures and the sober announcements of the continuing war in Europe and Asia. After the door closed behind him, Mother would walk into the dining room and turn the radio to WCCO, out of Minneapolis.

Then, back in the kitchen, she continued with her chores. As she washed dishes, I reached up to grab them. Then I rubbed them on both sides with a towel made from a flour sack. Dorothy was in her crib, close by the radio. It was just the three of us.

We worked and waited. Then a man's deep, deep voice floated to us. I'd never heard anybody speak like that man.

"This is Milton Cross. I'm coming to you live from New York City and the Metropolitan Opera House. And now [there'd be a long pause] the curtain is rising . . ."

And another world flowed from the dining room into the kitchen.

In my mind, I saw a room much larger than our church. Everyone was all dressed up. The man was speaking from the balcony in the rear, and all the men and women were facing forward as they listened.

If the opera was one that my mother was familiar with, she'd begin singing, making up the words she didn't know. When the singers soared off into musical heaven, I'd join in with nonsense words and notes. And there was one time when I heard noises from the corner where Dorothy lay in her crib. I spoke up over the music.

"Mommy," I said, "Dorothy likes opera, too!"

THE SPARE ROOM

⌐

In one stride, my father was across the room. His large hands grabbed my shoulders, and then, before I had a chance to say a word or cry out, he lifted me, holding me against his side, while he pulled out a kitchen chair and sat down on it. He threw me across his knees, and my breath went out in a sharp pain. My head swung down, and my blond hair swept the floor.

"Why do you always have to make such a racket? Screaming and yelling—that's all I hear when I walk into this house!"

Dad's hand hit my bottom hard, but before I could wonder how many more times he would do the same, I felt the liquid run along my leg. He pushed me off his knee and set me down.

I didn't feel any pain, only a terrible shame. As I ran out the door, I could see John and Bob trying not to smile.

The yard looked fuzzy to me, and I stumbled on the steps. I ran around the house and slid under the side of the porch. Our spirea bushes were in full bloom, their white blossoms falling in wide ribbons to the ground. It was a good place to hide, but the space was so low I couldn't sit up. I could only lie there and cry—cry until my throat burned and I felt the dry earth become mud on my hands and face.

I couldn't breathe. I wiggled out and, keeping my body close to the house, moved until I was just below the dining room window. Everyone was eating. The window was open a little, and I could smell fried onions. No one was talking. There was no laughter. Only the sounds of forks and knives on plates.

"Okay, let's get back to work, boys," I heard Dad say.

Chairs scraped against the floor.

"Bob, wait a minute." It was my mother's voice. "Go find Barbara. This has gone on long enough. Tell her I saved her a piece of pie."

I knew Bob would leave by the kitchen door, so I quickly moved back to the front of the house.

I slipped into the house quietly. My mother was in the kitchen, with her back turned, putting leftovers into small bowls. I tiptoed up the stairs, carefully avoiding the spot on the fifth step that always creaked. Slowly, quietly I crept down the hall and opened a door.

This was our "spare room." Although it had a bed and a dresser, it was never used as a bedroom. An old rocker with a gold velvet seat sat near the door. A small, battered black suitcase was nearby. This was filled with precious Christmas ornaments, and I was careful not to overturn it as I made my way to the bed in the corner. Winter clothes were piled on one end of the bed. At the other, a few faded blankets, their satin edges worn and loose, were stacked in a rough heap. I climbed onto the bed. My belly ached and my legs itched where my brown stockings had dried to them. I took the satin ribbon of a blanket and rubbed it on my check.

Black-and-white photographs of old people, the men with beards, the women in long skirts and blouses with high collars, gazed down on me from frames on the wall. I didn't recognize any of the faces. Not one of them smiled. They must have all been dead.

I'll just stay here until I die, I thought. *And then, when I get to heaven, I'll find Dorothy. It shouldn't be too hard. There can't be many cribs up in heaven. At least not with old kids in them. Dorothy will smile when she sees me. And then we'll wait. Wait until Mommy gets up there, too.*

SEEN AND NOT HEARD

⌐⁓

The nonstop calamities of the drought and the Great Depression, compounded by Dorothy's physical impairment (perhaps those two should be reversed), took their toll on my parents. And that toll fell, sometimes directly, on my siblings and me.

Their honeymoon period *was* short. Mother became pregnant within a month after they were married, and then, after Dorothy's birth, most of my mother's time and energy were divided between caring for her and performing endless housekeeping chores, for years without the aid of running water or electrical appliances. My father must have lost quite quickly the lighthearted young woman he'd married, as worry and work overwhelmed her. There would have been few smiles and little laughter.

My father coped by ignoring his emotional pain. My brother Bob, two years older than I, never heard him speak Dorothy's name, nor did I.

Relatives told my siblings and me that as a young man, my father had a playful side and always spoke with pride of how he and his college mates managed to coax a cow up the steps of Old North, the tallest academic building on campus. Three

narrow flights up! I never heard whether the college adminis-
trators figured out who the culprits were—or how they got the
poor cow down.

I heard an echo of that younger man one Sunday morning.
It was a tradition that our cow's prized rich cream accompanied
us to church. Mother prepared the liquid gold by pouring it into
a blue Mason jar. As the youngest, I was responsible for carrying
the jar to the rectory and giving it to Miss Olivia, the priest's
housekeeper. She, in turn, would place two quarters and a dime
in the palm of my hand.

One Sunday morning, we were later than usual. I wanted to
join my family in our pew before Mass started. Everyone would
stare at me if I came in late. As soon as my father stopped the
car, I threw open my door, grabbed the jar, and ran up a small
slope, but my foot caught on the edge of the sidewalk and I went
tumbling. I wasn't hurt, but the jar broke, and I began to cry as
the stream of cream widened. I knew how much work had been
necessary to produce that quart of cream, and how much that
sixty cents meant.

My father was there almost immediately. I caught my
breath. I tried to stop crying and waited for the announcement
of the punishment to come.

I was surprised when my father said only, "Don't cry over
spilt milk."

I heard him chuckle a bit at the aptness of the situation. I
didn't look at him, afraid that doing so might change his mood.

"I'm sorry," I mumbled, as I followed my mother up the
church steps.

The central tenet of parents in our community was "children
should be seen, not heard." They were first- or second-generation
Americans, primarily from Central Europe and Scandinavia.
Children were to be useful, help with the chores, and, above all,
not make any disturbances.

So my father's behavior was the norm. When one of us
disobeyed, my father spanked. My siblings say that I escaped
that form of punishment. I did not. But I never felt the belt.
One day Patt, who always had a keen sense of justice and who

certainly was the bravest of all of us, did the unthinkable. After deciding that my father was resorting to using that instrument too often, she hid it! I can't imagine that her action improved my father's disposition.

NEVER MEANT TO BE
A FARMER

‿‿‿‿↘

My father was never meant to be a farmer. He held a Bach-elor of Science degree in a time and a place where even obtaining a high school diploma was a distinction. There were a doctor and a lawyer in Ortonville, but the superintendent of schools, our pastor, and my father were the only Big Stone res-idents who'd earned a degree.

His father, who'd emigrated from Denmark and learned English on his own, made great sacrifices so that his oldest son could attend high school and then college. My father majored in chemistry and, after graduating, accepted a teaching position in the tiny town of Ree Heights so that he could be near my mother, who'd moved back to her hometown of Pierre, some sixty miles away.

My mother had not been his first love. I learned of that one summer day.

Home from college, I asked about a ring I saw in my mother's jewelry box. She said that it was to have been given to another woman, whom my father had met while he was at college. This was during World War I. My father had been a

78

member of the Student Army Training Corps in high school. Immediately following graduation, he was sent to South Dakota State College for further training. Then the Spanish flu hit. My father survived that tragic time when hundreds fell ill and entire dormitories were turned into infirmaries, but many of his friends did not, including the young woman he'd fallen in love with and planned to marry.

Obviously, my father had given my mother the ring meant for another. As far as I know, neither woman ever wore it. When she told me the story, my mother seemed to exhibit no resentment, only sorrow at the loss of such a young life. We know our parents met at college, but whether they met before or after the tragedy remains unknown.

Mother gave the ring to me, but I didn't have it resized, and I also never wore it. Feeling as if the passage of time had dissipated the sadness associated with the ring, I eventually gave it to a niece, who wore it as her "something old" on her wedding day.

The only clue I have into my parents' early relationship is jotted in my mother's hand in one of those capture-your-memories-before-you-die books. "Was it love at first sight?" it asked her. She wrote, "No."

The memoir-writer me has so many questions and wishes I had pushed her to tell me more. The daughter me is glad I didn't.

What happened in Ree Heights, that little town sixty miles east of Pierre, set the course of my parents' lives. My father accepted a position at the high school there, teaching math and chemistry. One of his students happened to be the son of a school board member. That son was either dumb or lazy or both. For the first term, my father gave him a D in math. During the last term, the time when teacher contracts were renewed, the student's father demanded that my father raise his son's grade.

"If his work improves, I will," my father replied.

The student's work did not improve, and my father failed the student. His contract was not renewed.

The next year, he managed to find a position in New England, North Dakota. The town was a little larger than Ree Heights, but my father was miserable. It was located much farther from Pierre and the woman he loved. My grandfather was planning a trip back to Denmark to visit his family, the first and only time he made that journey after immigrating to America, and my father offered to manage the farm in his father's absence.

It seemed appropriate that my father stay on there after my parents got married. My grandfather generously offered to lease his house and his farm on the banks of the Whetstone River.

Passage of the Homestead Act in South Dakota in 1862 fueled the settlement of the state. Pioneers were granted ownership of the land, typically 160 acres, after farming it for five years. My grandfather had filed papers for his sister, Ella. (The document is signed by Theodore Roosevelt and dated 1905.) After my parents moved to our farmhouse, he and my grandmother settled into the smaller house on that property on the prairie-like fields northwest of Big Stone City.

No part of my parents' courtship could have been easy. My mother was a Catholic of French-Canadian descent. (Her ancestors fought under Montcalm in the Battle of Quebec, and her grandfather traded with Indians at the time of Lewis and Clark's great exploits.) My father was a Lutheran, one generation removed from Protestant Scandinavia. And Big Stone City was composed of a great divide: Catholics versus Protestants.

What conversations did my parents have about this important issue? My mother was devout; she would have been unyielding. My father converted to Catholicism. At that time, their union would have caused an uproar, similar to the tempests surrounding interracial marriages in the 1950s.

In our town, Catholics and Protestants viewed each other warily. The respective houses of worship were off-limits to nonmembers; Protestants didn't attend weddings or funerals of Catholic neighbors, and vice versa. The town minister was even known to cross to the other side of the street while walking, to avoid meeting the priest. By the time I was old enough to be aware of these relationships, this division had been eased because of the masterful diplomatic skills of Father Esterguard, who, as soon as he was assigned to our parish, reached out to Catholics, Protestants, and nonbelievers alike.

My father became a farmer in fact but never in spirit. He refused to wear the eminently practical bib overalls, de rigueur uniform of that occupation. He approached farming with a scientist's eye, meticulously tracking the quality of milk his Holsteins produced in order to perfect the herd. To aid him in calculating the amount of fertilizer to be used, he sent corn samples to be tested at the state lab. He became the first farmer in the county to rotate his crops. He subscribed to *South Dakota Conservation Digest*, following an early interest; his essay entitled "National Conservation" was selected to be read at his high school commencement in 1917. And, although he was not naturally mechanical, using ingenuity, he fixed the farm machinery. But my father had no enthusiasm for the day-to-day care of animals or the repetitious labor of field work. Rather, he loved to experiment, to plan, to devise, to act. Alas, he was trying to earn a living in a way that was mostly tedious, boring, and disappointing.

My father was offered a chance to escape that drudgery. In 1941, the US government was recruiting men who weren't eligible to serve in the armed services to aid in the war effort, including bright minds to support brilliant ones. My father was "requested" to use the knowledge he'd gained in college and take a position at a chemical company located near Chicago. Later, he learned that the company was supporting the Manhattan Project, which developed the first nuclear weapons. In talking about this to Bob, my father said the pressure for him to accept the job was intense, so much so that my father, who rivaled Lincoln in his honesty ethos (Abe supposedly walked six miles to return a three-cent overcharge), told my brother, "I almost had to lie." Somehow he managed to sidestep the dilemma.

When I heard this story in 2012, I assumed that my father had declined the offer because of the difficulty that moving a household of seven children would have entailed.

"No, that wasn't it," he told Bob in his later years. "I just couldn't tear you kids away. You would have been lost without the river."

My father was without sentiment and had no patience for superstition or ignorance. He was practical to a frustrating degree.

When I complained that he'd driven over a patch of wild purple asters at the edge of a field, he fired back, "What? Those are weeds!"

When I objected, he answered with his maxim, "Any flower growing where it doesn't belong is a weed."

He could be blunt when talking about a person's frailties, and seemed to have no concern for the feelings of his children. My father's telling of the latest confrontation in the ongoing feud with the neighbor woman enlivened many of our supper conversations. He seemed to cultivate his dislike of this woman, his cousin's wife, Irene, who was a new arrival from Minneapolis. She had an outspoken nature and didn't fit in with the local standards of what a woman "should" be, and that rankled my father. Sometimes it seemed he believed women, like children, ought to be seen and not heard.

Irene considered herself an authority on certain matters on which my father *was* an authority. He didn't like being told he was wrong, especially when he wasn't. That characteristic of hers probably would have been enough to put her on his bad side, but when she began acquiring land—not acres, just pieces and bits, so that her property now abutted ours in a few places—my father's remarks became more caustic.

The final blow was when she bought land on both sides of "our" road to Big Stone City, and with it, in her mind, the road itself. She knew that it was our family's only way to drive to town.

The original county road had been washed out some twenty years earlier. "Our" road may not have been registered at the courthouse, but it had been used as such. My father, accompanied by neighbors, met with officials who decided that after all those years of usage, the road was considered in the public domain.

Without that decision, our family would have been forced to drive up a much steeper hill, and my siblings and I to take a longer, more difficult route when we walked to school.

Of course, he brought his strong opinions and tenacity with him when he served on the school board, as a member, then president. During his tenure, he oversaw the design and construction of a second school building to accommodate the growing number of students. Meetings often devolved into shouting matches, but my father persisted. An attractive, simple, one-story building was constructed. His name, etched on a granite plaque near the entry, still attests to his perseverance.

More and more often, as my brothers grew in years and strength, my father found reasons why a trip off the farm and into town was a necessity for him. He'd drive to town, pick up the mail, and walk across the street to the little café. There, he would catch up on the latest news and roll dice with the locals to determine who was to pick up the tab for the five-cents-per-cup coffee.

When our cows had once again found a gap in the fences and were out on the highway, in desperation my mother would call the telephone operator in Big Stone. More than once, that patient woman put down her headphones and abandoned her switchboard, dashed across the street to the café, and told my father he was urgently needed at home.

After the flood destroyed the white wooden bridge, county officials sought a less costly way to replace it. They decided that installing giant, galvanized steel culverts covered with packed dirt would be cheaper. The structure, ugly and utilitarian, would allow my father and brothers to go back and forth to the South Field and all of us to get to neighboring farms to share chores and companionship.

But those officials underestimated the power of the runoff from the melting snow, even in an ordinary year. Within two years, the packed dirt and the gravel topping were beginning to break away. In three years, all the dirt was gone, leaving us with three ugly, useless culverts. Now we had to resort to fording, just as the pioneers had done long before. I'd jump from gravel at the river's edge to a large stone to the next large stone as I made my way to visit my friend MaryLee. When my father and brothers set out to tend to the crops, they carefully drove through the shallows below these rocks. If the water was too deep, they had to drive the tractor to the edge of town with a plow, a disc, or a hay mower, depending on the season, hitched behind it, and continue more than a mile on the highway and then on country roads in order to approach the fields from the opposite direction—a frustrating expenditure of time and gas. But even when the river was relatively low, unexpected problems could arise.

Bob tells the story.

Dad had been harvesting the last of the corn on that unseasonably warm October day when he came storming into the yard, his work clothes dripping with water and his face, always red from years in the sun, redder than ever.

"Those damn beavers!" my father yelled.

Beavers—those storybook creatures with their endearing buckteeth—can cause a lot of damage in a short time. They must have worked especially hard the previous night, because they'd raised their dam high enough that when my father drove the tractor across the river at the usual spot, water splashed into it, short-circuiting the engine.

"Grab the dynamite!" he yelled to Bob. "We're going to wipe those bastards out!"

As Bob tells me about that day, he explains, "We *always* had dynamite on hand to move really heavy things."

Taking a dynamite cap and fuses, they hiked downriver, where they discovered that their enemies had built a dam some four feet high. Dad fused the dynamite sticks; Bob placed them at three-foot intervals along the length of the dam. Then he lit another one, which he tossed toward the end of the string. He covered his ears and waited, as was customary, to make sure it would "take" and thus ignite the other sticks. Nothing happened, so he repeated the process. That time it worked; they were just beginning to walk away when the first mud began to fly.

"Run!" one—or both—of them yelled.

They took refuge behind an old elm tree, but just then a strong wind blew in and they were bombarded with stick and stone-laden mud. When the air had settled, they looked at each other. They were covered with the brown stuff but unhurt.

"Guess we forgot to factor in the wind," my father said.

The beavers never rebuilt in that location.

OTHER BRIDGES

The white bridge had been vital to our family, but other bridges, too, were an integral part of our life. To get to school, we walked up our drive, along a dirt road for about a mile, and crossed over US Highway 12, after briefly pausing for a semi truck and a car or two to pass by. Then we turned left and crossed a wide-board wooden bridge, taking a minute to peer through the slats of the railing to the tracks below. The smell of creosote-soaked railway ties wafted up.

After we crossed the bridge, there was a decision to be made: Take the shortcut or not? It would save us fifteen minutes, but we'd have to outwit the nasty dog that belonged to the owner of a nearby house. The dog would begin barking as soon as he caught sight of us, chase after us, and bite our heels if we didn't run fast enough. The end of the shortcut brought us to the street directly across from school. If my brothers were with me, I braved the dog, but if I was alone, I never tried to go that way but rather continued on the street, passing by a few small houses with small yards, for another quarter of a mile to the red brick schoolhouse.

The cars of the Chicago, Milwaukee, & St. Paul Railway ran under that bridge. A half mile farther along, the bridge that had been rerouted to the edge of our property, the bridge that changed the channel, spanned the river. When that railroad line was completed, a person could climb aboard in Ortonville and travel all the way to Seattle without stepping off.

When a train passed through our town and crossed country roads, the engineer activated the whistle by pulling a cord. As I lay in bed, those haunting, musical sounds carried through the still night air to our house, reminding me that other people were on the move, traveling through prairies and mountains and forests, all the way to the ocean's edge.

CALLING THE COWS HOME

ⵑ

At various times, my father raised chickens, guinea hens, pigs, and sheep. He kept a couple of horses even after a John Deere tractor had replaced their work, but the other creatures came and went. They would be there for a few years, and then no more, as market prices fluctuated and they were deemed more effort than their worth.

Labrador retrievers (both black and golden) were treasured as loyal hunting partners, and dogs of indiscriminate breeds earned their way working as herders. My father tolerated, barely, the barn cats because they kept the rodent population in check.

In turn, oldest to youngest, my siblings and I left the farm. But his herd of Holstein cows remained a constant during all those years. My father appreciated them as he did no other species.

"We had the best-producing herd in the state of South Dakota one month when testing with the Dairy Herd Improvement Association," he wrote in a brief self-history.

Reading this now, I hear his voice when he talked to Bessie, the lead cow—the boss—of the herd, in an encouraging you-can-do-it tone. And, although at times my brothers must have been the ones to call the cows in from the pasture to be milked, it's my father's voice, his cadence, I hear now, drawing out the phrase "c'm boss, ca' boss . . ."

"Go get 'em," he ordered the current dog. And the dog ran off to locate the herd.

I waited along with my father. It was beginning to get dark. We could hear the dog yipping.

"Ca' boss, ca' boss."

The sound of his voice lingered in the cool air.

We heard a responding low "mooo," and then we saw movement beneath the low branches of the oak trees. Slowly, Bessie and her reluctant followers left the pasture and, single file, splashed noisily through the shallows and trudged to the gate. Where my father waited.

LOOKING FOR COLOR

Nature doled out color meagerly during the long winter months. The sky at times seemed as dormant as the earth. No rainbows, no northern lights, no slashes of lightning that came with the summer heat.

The trees were dull and naked. The old, barren cottonwood, with no leaves to add their tinkling melody, stood silent. Wildflowers, grasses, weeds, mosses all lay withered beneath the snow.

I struggled to keep up with my older brothers on the way to school. We were always hurrying. They'd gotten up at six-thirty to milk our cows before returning to the house to wash up and change clothes. Clomping down the steps, they yelled to me to get my coat on or I'd be left behind.

As we passed the frozen slough, I'd try to catch a glimpse of the lone kinnikinnick bush. In winter, its bare branches were a resonant red, which stood out amid the dreary reeds at the edge. My mother taught me to appreciate the kinnikinnick bush because of its vivid color. Later I learned that early Native Americans appreciated it, too. Its name is *cha-shasha* (redwood) in Dakota Sioux. After removing the outer bark, members of the tribe scraped and dried the inner bark. Then they smoked it. Because the bark is especially fragrant, all the tribes coveted it.

When it was very cold or my brothers were late coming in from the barn, our father would reluctantly concede to drive us to school. I'd climb in and try to hold my place in the backseat, right behind my father. That way, I'd be on the slough side. Too often, that didn't matter because the car windows would be covered by heavy frost, but when all went well I'd catch glints of red flashing between the tans and browns.

Our school clothes were drab and colorless, too. Sometimes I wore hand-me-downs, the material being used for the garment's third incarnation by the time it got to me. Originally the skirts had been cut and sewn from adult clothing for my sisters. When they outgrew them, they were put in a closet and years later brought out for me. In those days, girls didn't wear slacks; leggings didn't even exist. So, all through the winter months, I was forced to wear long cotton stockings beneath my skirts. Hours before lunch, the brown garments hung baggy around my knees. My shoes were an almost-matching ugly brown.

In winter, without the red strawberries and tomatoes and the green beans and peas from our garden, our food, with a few exceptions, was colorless as well. After my father had butchered a steer, my mother made a soup with the hocks. She added potatoes and carrots and, at the very end some cabbage. The carrots were stored in the basement in an old milk can filled with sand so they would remain crisp throughout the winter. Chunks of orange carrots and green strips of cabbage floated in the neutral-colored broth.

When we attended Mass, I looked forward to its pageantry and music. But during long, incomprehensible sermons, I found ways to entertain myself. Without wiggling, which would have brought a stern rebuke from my father, I'd try to find all the gold surfaces. They brightened as the candle flames flickered.

The priest wore shiny silk embroidered with more silk, which shimmered when he genuflected. His vestments were colorful, always a hue decreed by the church calendar. I understood none of that, but as my young years crept along I became aware that when the priest donned the purple for Advent, the best days of the year were not far away.

Christmas brought anticipation and excitement, special food prepared—and consumed—in great quantities, adults playing cards and telling stories, all of us laughing more than at any other time of the year.

Christmas *was* color. We trimmed our tree with multicolored lights, small balls, miniature cherubs, and silver cones with delicate openings that we hung point end down over the lights. Then we added crinkled strips of silver tinsel. My sisters and older brothers took the top branches, Bob and I the lower.

Every Christmas, our dear Aunt Marian battled winter weather on her long drive from Pierre. When she unpacked her suitcase, there'd be gifts for each one of us that she'd chosen with care to reflect our ages and personalities. Wrapping paper printed with snowy scenes, reindeer, and fishing gear fueled our anticipation.

In preparation for the holiday, our mother labored into the nights, baking fruitcakes and pies, sweet rolls and bread, jelly rolls and cookies. Bob and I were enlisted to set the table. After we'd put the leaves in place and covered the table with the felt protector, we took out the giant white damask tablecloth from the long drawer of the buffet. After ironing it, Mother had carefully rolled it around a very long cardboard tube so there would be no creases. We laid it on the table and struggled to make all the sides even.

Then Bob would take off out the door to catch up with our brothers, and I was on my own. My mother's silver was stored in a tarnish-resistant cloth that was rolled and tied. I untied the bow and laid the bundle flat. I took each piece out of its own small compartment, often pausing to admire the delicate patterns in the light, and began to set the table.

I opened the door at the side of the buffet and, one by one, took out the etched crystal goblets and placed them just so, as my mother had taught me. Later, as we passed the laden serving dishes around the table, the water in the beautiful glasses would jiggle a bit. Then the bright red color of the cranberry sauce and the pickled beets contrasted beautifully with the white cloth.

When I was fourteen, I found myself alone one day as I was weeding the garden and a traveling salesman pulled up to our house. I was the perfect customer. He didn't even have to knock on our door, and no one else was there when he made his pitch.

This was at a time when teenagers my age who lived on farms could obtain a driver's permit, an exception to the norm, so that they could drive farm equipment on the highways. And with that piece of paper tucked into the glove compartment of my father's car, I was able to get a job at the drive-in theater, where I worked in the concession stand. I received not just coins but a paycheck—social security withheld and all.

So the salesman found me at just the right time. I had money to spend. He talked me into a layaway plan for a silverware set. The starter was a one-piece setting in a chest, which I would receive in a few weeks. And there was no charge for the chest!

I accumulated place setting by place setting until my older brother Bill found out. He was born, it seems, with an acute business sense.

"Why are you spending money on silverware? At your age. You won't be using it for years! If you'd invest that money instead, it would accrue interest. Your money would earn money that you can use for college. You'd have that, not some shiny stuff just sitting in a chest!"

Of course he was right—I didn't use the silverware, but still I treasured it and enjoyed knowing that I owned something beautiful, as my mother did.

Many years later, when my parents were about to move into a care facility, my mother handed me her original set of silver, the one I'd loved setting the table with. At that time, I was a mother of only one son.

"In time you'll pass this on to Peter, won't you?" my mother asked.

"Yes, of course. I promise."

When our second son, Stephen, was about to be married, I gave Katee, his bride, the set the salesman had sold me. Before wrapping it with gift paper, I opened the chest and lifted out a spoon. For the first time, I noticed how closely the pattern of my silver resembled my mother's.

A MATTER OF FAITH

Like the weather, religion was woven through our lives. Each Sunday morning, we got up, got dressed, and without breakfast—an empty stomach was required to receive communion—went to Mass. There were no alternatives. No way to preempt that early hour by attending Mass late Saturday afternoon or early Sunday evening, as is possible today. And the incentive was great. It was a mortal sin to miss Sunday Mass—meaning you were damned to hell if you didn't manage to make it to confession before your demise.

The same rule held for Holy Days, which often fell on weekdays. Those mornings, we had to get up even earlier. The time for Mass on Holy Days was set so that businessmen would be able to open their doors at the usual hour and schoolchildren would be on time for roll call. As a young child, I found it exciting and a bit spooky to be awakened in the dark, get dressed, and climb into the car while the stars were still bright in the sky.

Midway through the liturgy of the Mass, following the Gospel, the priest delivered the weekly sermon. Those that revolved around the Old Testament, especially the stories about Job, with his endless trials and tribulations, seemed to reflect our family's reality.

And for any enterprising priest in that area, there was rich sermon material in recounting the plagues of Egypt. Hail, though not fiery, as stated in the Bible, brought destruction to area farms, demolishing a season's work in a matter of minutes. Then add these: drought, dust storms, high winds, tornadoes, grasshoppers, sleeping-horse disease, blight, early frosts, and, especially for us, living as we were on the banks of the Whetstone River, floods.

During the growing season, Sunday Mass seemed to drag on and on. The church was stifling hot without air-conditioning. Tall stained-glass windows were spaced evenly along each side of the building. A small panel at the bottom of each beautiful window would be cranked open. Lucky was the person seated at the end of a pew near a window. That person was always an adult. Kids were sandwiched between parents.

Through those narrow openings, scents of grass and wild clover filtered in, along with a few flies and box elder bugs. Those bugs gathered in great clusters on the sides of buildings every August. When viewed up close, they displayed an art deco design of slate gray and orange, accented by protruding red eyes. These annoying creatures created dilemmas for grown-ups (and entertainment for us kids) as they slowly crawled up the back of the person seated in the pew ahead. To brush the bug off or let it continue its slow ascent? The first action would disturb the unaware person, perhaps jarring him from a short snooze. No action would eventually lead to a startled jump as the bug advanced to the person's skin, followed by a conspicuous whack that sent the insect to the floor. The bug-laden person would hope to accomplish this final act of the mini drama without disturbing the priest's exaltations.

At every Sunday Mass from the beginning of May to the end of August, prayers for a good harvest were added to the service just before the sermon. Priests never omitted those prayers; the welfare of their parishes was as dependent on the quality and quantity of the crops just as much as it was for members of the congregation. Everyone responded to those intercessions the priest voiced with fervent intensity.

In 2017, as I was sorting through old papers, I found a little leaflet of those prayers. I decided to time them. A friend took the priest's role, calling on the individual saints. I took the part of the parishioners, appealing to those holy ones for mercy.

"St. Stephen."

"Pray for us."

"St. Lawrence."

"Pray for us."

"St. Vincent."

"Pray for us."

"All ye holy martyrs."

"Pray for us."

And so we continued, calling out saint after saint, twelve more, until the end. We spoke the prayers at the pace at which I remember their being said in our church—that is, rapidly. Even so, it took us a full ten minutes to complete the series. At that point, the essential parts of the service were still to come. After a recitation of the Creed of the Apostles, there was the Offertory, followed by Communion. None of this would be hurried. So when the priest finally dismissed us with a rumbling "Go in peace," we were ready to bolt out into the fresh air.

RETURNING TO CHURCH

Might it have been my mother's announcement to my father that she was expecting? Pregnant again, that time with me. Was that the push that tumbled my father into nonbelief? Even though it was a mortal sin to miss Sunday Mass, at some point my father had stopped going to church with us.

And was it I, a few years later, who caused him to reassess his faith?

After my father's funeral, which was held in our parish church, my sisters talked to me about this.

"You were the one who brought Dad back to the Church," they told me. There was something like awe in their voices.

"Mother became very unhappy when Dad stayed home Sunday after Sunday," Helen said.

"He always said he didn't have enough time, that there was too much work to be done," Patt said. "He used that same excuse for years."

"What did I do? What did I say?" I asked my sisters. I would have been about five at that time.

Neither could offer an answer or any details, and I have no memory of it. No matter what tactic I had used to persuade my father to once again go to church, the three of us recognized that doing so would have required a great deal of resolve on his part. To "return," he first had to go to confession. "Bless me father, for I have sinned. It's been [fill in the blank] years since my last confession." Then he'd have to list all of the sins that he'd committed during the intervening years. And, according to church doctrine at that time, almost *everything* was a sin, and not attending Sunday Mass was a grievous sin, a mortal sin.

In the airless cubicle, a screen separated the sinner from the priest. Privacy was an illusion. In our small parish, the priest recognized every voice. Of course he knew it was Roy Hoffbeck who knelt only a few inches from him on the other side of the screen. And, of course, my father knew that the priest knew.

It's unknown what turned my father away or what I might have done that gave him the impetus to return, but I'm sure it was his love for my mother that gave him the courage. He must have realized he possessed the power to erase one of her sorrows.

So, one Saturday evening, in an unknown season of an unknown year, he parked the car, climbed the steps, and opened the heavy wooden door of the church. George Esterguard was the priest on the other side of the screen, waiting to hear my father's confession. After he had listed his sins, Father Esterguard's words would have been gentle, his counsel spoken carefully, and the penance he pronounced one that could be accomplished easily. As my father exited the confessional, each of the men, parishioner and priest, would have felt unencumbered and free of a great weight.

In preparation for my First Communion, I'd been required to confess my sins aloud to the priest during my First Reconciliation. It was on a summer day some years after that when the same priest sat on the other side of the screen from me. I was only just beginning to understand the church and its teachings. Each Sunday, I'd listened to the sermons, which often focused on the Ten Commandments. Some of the commandments were easy to understand: "Thou shall honor your mother and your father." "Thou shall not kill." A few of them less so: "Thou shall not commit adultery." "Thou shall not covet thy neighbor's wife."

I was probably only six at the time of my nightmare confession. I was very scared but determined to tell the truth. Something I'd done was terrible, something that had to be confessed, something that could send me to hell. It now seems as if I were baptized with water and sprinkled with guilt.

I wanted to get rid of the terrible feeling that followed me through each day. After my sisters had made their confessions and returned to the pew we were sharing, I walked to the back of the church, pushed back the heavy velvet curtain, entered, and knelt. I would be brave. I would tell the priest my horrible sin.

"Bless me, Father, for I have sinned. It has been two weeks since my last confession. I fought with my brothers."

I was stalling. Finally, I continued, "I have committed"—I concentrated on saying the next word correctly—"adultery."

My announcement was followed by silence, probably the longest pause in the history of confessions. I could hardly breathe. I waited for a terrible scolding and a never-ending penance. I realize now that the silence probably indicated that Father Esterguard was trying very hard not to laugh.

Listening to a Sunday sermon, I must have misunderstood one of the priest's pronouncements. My child's mind had conflated innocent play with a sinful act.

One day, my friend MaryLee and I had been splashing around in the shallows near the Little Rock when we'd decided it'd be fun to take our swimsuits off. Staying below the water, we put our suits under rocks to keep them from being carried away by the current. When we decided to leave the river and return to the house, in the process of retrieving our suits, we stood up. Then we heard my brothers calling out to us from farther up the river. They'd seen us naked!

As I knelt in the confessional, my stomach ached. I waited.

At last, the priest spoke: "Say ten Our Fathers and ten Hail Marys." And with that, he blessed and dismissed me.

"Go in peace," he said, as he closed the screen.

A WIDER WORLD

"Can I ride to town with you?" I asked my father. "Please." When I was not yet two, I left the house and followed my father to the barn. He didn't see me until I walked up right behind a cow. With a swoop, he pulled me away before a high-powered hoof could have done me in. My mother told me that the spanking I received did nothing to change my inclination to venture out and discover.

A few years later, I began to pester my father to allow me to ride to town with him.

"Please!"

It was a fine line. If I went from asking to begging, he'd definitely say no.

This happened only in late fall or during the winter, when the fields were frozen hard. When I was four, my siblings, including my brother Bob, who was my coadventurer, were off at school. I was bored. I had one hand-me-down doll and was good at make-believe, but I had no one to play with.

Usually my father said no, but when he did agree, I got to sit up front. This in itself was exciting. It was the only chance I ever got to ride in that important spot. My view, of course, was not straight ahead—I was too short for that—but out the side window. Down the drive, up the hill, down the other side, past the slough and a small, still-green field, and then up the sand hill. All the time, my father was doing fun things with his feet and the pedals while his hand was pushing the shift this way and that.

We came to a stop, and he looked back and forth before he turned down the big road to town. He always parked in front of the post office. Sometimes he helped me out of the car and let me tag along. The inside of the post office had rows and rows of small boxes trimmed in gold with glass windows, and a man sitting in a cage. My father and that man talked about the weather. Our box was numbered 516. Once, my father lifted me up so I could put the small key into the tiny slot and swing the door open.

Next, he headed to the grocery store. My father always said good morning to Mr. Lauster, who stood behind a counter. They talked about the weather, and then my father told him what my mother needed. It was usually only a few items, things we didn't grow on the farm, maybe baking powder or vanilla. Then we waited as the man went to shelves behind him and picked out the items. My father signed his name on a small piece of paper, gathered the things up, and said, "Thank you! Goodbye."

After he put those things in the car, my father took my hand and we crossed the large road to a little restaurant. It was smoky and noisy inside. Men sat on tall stools at the counter. They moved around to make room for the two of us. Even before my father sat down, the waitress had already brought him a cup of coffee. With a smile, she handed me a cookie. I took small bites to make my treat last longer. The men talked about the weather.

I realize now that after we left the cafe, both of us had hated to get into the car. At home, chores waited for him, as they did for me. Back in front of our house, I'd hear him sigh as he turned off the engine.

"Now, go in and help your mother," he'd say.

My chores were limited because of my strength and my height, but I brought up jars of canned food from the cellar, set the table, swept, and, of course, did the most boring job of all: dusting. A small, stand-alone bookcase in the corner of the living room held a few grown-up books and a ten-volume set of *The Book of Knowledge.*

The man who sold that set to my parents must have been a very enterprising salesperson. He'd been able to find his way down the unmarked road to our house, and, once there, somehow he'd convinced my parents they could manage the payments.

At the bookcase, I'd stop dusting and curl myself in close to the wall where I couldn't be seen. I'd pick up one volume and then another, flipping the pages at random and studying the black-and-white photographs. Time would drift away. I was no longer a little girl on a farm. I was wearing an embroidered skirt and jacket and herding reindeer. I was in a very dry place, pounding kernels of corn on a large, flat stone. I was far, far away. Until, that is, my father would come in and see my mother working alone in the kitchen.

His booming voice made me jump.

"Where's Barbara? Why isn't she out here helping you?"

I'd jump up, quickly gather the dustcloth, and move to an area where he could see me work.

It was that urge to see more of the world that got me into trouble shortly after my ninth birthday. It was unusually warm that fall, and my father had planned a hunting trip. Overnight! A first. My brothers and he were going "west of the river." They always spoke those words a little differently. They'd drive a long way before they crossed the Missouri River to wide-open spaces. There, they'd hunt for grouse.

My brothers called back and forth as they packed the car. Our two Labrador retrievers jumped around excitedly. There was no way they were going to be left behind.

My father sat drinking a final cup of coffee while Mother wrapped sandwiches in waxed paper. She and I would be left alone, our feet the only mode of transportation.

"This isn't fair! I never get to go anywhere!" I said.

"What! You have such an easy life. And you're complaining?" my father replied.

"But I never get to go anywhere!"

My father began to push back his chair. I didn't see his face, but I saw something in the hunch of his shoulders.

I didn't hesitate. I ran out the door, letting it slam shut, across the yard, swung open the gate to the horse pasture, not bothering to latch it behind me, and just kept going. Fear pushed me. I picked up speed as I ran down the slope and across the top of the Big Rock.

"Barbara! Stop! Stop right now!"

From there, tall, wilted weeds and brown grasses made it almost impossible for me to see the path. But I knew it by heart. I didn't slow down even when I felt thorns catching on my clothes and scratching my arms. My father was so close, I could hear his feet thud-thud-thudding on the dirt. I'd never seen my father run. I didn't know he could.

Then I reached the barbed-wire fence.

He was right behind me, about to grab my blouse. Just in time, I dropped to the ground and rolled under the lowest rung of the spiky wire fence.

I knew that it would take him a few minutes before he could separate and hold the two middle wires apart to step through the fence. In that short time, I'd be able to run through the corn rows and find a place to hide. By the time he could fetch the dogs and begin searching for me, I'd already have crossed the field to the highway.

My father was on one side of the fence. I was on the other. He was panting. I was crying.

"If you come home, I won't spank you," he said.

I stood there, tears running down my face.

"I mean it. If you come home, I won't punish you. But now. I mean *now!*" With that, he turned and walked away.

I hesitated. He continued walking. I watched him until he reached the Big Rock, until I couldn't see him anymore. Then I slipped back under the fence. When I opened the door to our house, I didn't look at anyone, not even Mother. I went to the stairs, up to my room, fell on my bed, and began to sob.

Only when I heard the car move away did I go downstairs.

There I looked out the window and watched as the dust slowly settled back down on our driveway.

It was very quiet that evening, both inside the house and out in the yard. No father, no brothers, no dogs. I was very tired and got ready for bed early.

In the morning, my uncle Earl came down to milk the cows, as he had the evening before. Then Mother and I went to the barn, my mother to wash the separator, I to feed the cats.

When we returned to the house, Mother went to the kitchen. I wandered into the living room, where I sat on the couch, swinging my legs back and forth. After a time, Mother came to the doorway.

"Come. We're going on our own adventure."

I looked up. She was wearing an old white shirt of my father's, as though she were going to work in the garden, and held a brown paper bag in her hand.

We walked down the driveway, across the white bridge, and continued toward the South Hill. When we reached the wild plum thicket, she climbed through the barbed-wire fence. Then she held the strands apart for me and I stepped through. We walked westward along the side of the hill.

Soon I was in new territory! I'd never been here before. How had Bob and I not discovered this place?

The dull browns of weeds and brambles changed to green. Everything was lush. A small spring ran over rocks covered in patches of yellowish green. Near the water, short grass, the color of peas, grew in spiky clumps. Moss that covered the rocks along the edge of the water was brilliant green; it seemed to glow in the dim light. High above us, brown leaves, still holding fast to the oak trees, moved gently.

Mother and I stood on the steep slope with one foot below the other. We scouted for a large rock, and when we found one, to avoid its sharp bumps, we sat close together in a scoop of its surface. We were looking in the direction of our yard and our house but couldn't see them. It was as though they'd disappeared.

Mother opened the bag and gave me a ham sandwich, and from a blue glass jar she poured lemonade. After we finished our sandwiches, we folded the waxed paper. Then she handed me two chocolate chip cookies. I thought she'd given the whole batch to my father and brothers!

We didn't talk. We just listened to the music that the water made as it tumbled over the rocks, down the hill to the river.

I never tried to find that spot again. I'm not sure why, but I'm glad I didn't, because this way it stays as it was when my mother and I picnicked there, the emerald-green moss clinging to the rocks, the song of the water as it slipped down its narrow channel, the oak leaves on the branches shielding my eyes, and my mind, from what had happened the day before.

TRYING TO FIT IN

～

Working to fit in and trying to please were the elusive quests of my girlhood. After Helen and Patt had left home, my father continued to dominate. As my brothers grew, so did their value, and with that my father began to take their opinions seriously. Not so with me. My brothers had plenty of opportunities to bond with him—not only while working, but also while hunting and fishing.

My brothers always gathered up their hunting gear with a sense of purpose and expectancy. Bob, who began hunting alone when he was ten, was doing that one January Sunday afternoon. It had snowed the day before, producing ideal conditions for tracking animals. Our parents were half reading, half sleeping in the living room. There was nothing for me to do.

"Bob, what are you going to hunt?"

"Anything that moves."

"Can I go with you?"

I could tell he enjoyed this moment. He held a position of power, something he never experienced when he worked with our father or John and Bill. He kept me waiting.

"Well, okay, but bundle up. It's cold out there."

I knew that. We'd returned from church only a couple of hours before. The two of us walked up the drive and then set out onto the field. The snow was deep so that no weeds or grasses broke through the surface. Out in the field, yesterday afternoon's warming temperatures had melted the top layer of the snow; colder temperatures at night had refrozen it so that now there was a thin crust. Our feet made crunching sounds as we broke through the glittering top. I trudged behind Bob. He held up his hand. I stopped.

On that January afternoon, I never thought he'd try to kill a rabbit. When I was very little, our father had brought a bunny in from the field. He explained that the nest had been hidden in the alfalfa that he'd been cutting. Its mother had been killed by the mower's blades. Bob and I loved touching the tiny animal's soft fur. We could feel its heart beating rapidly. We found an old shoe box and then went out to the yard, where we pulled blades of new grass and lined the box. Mother gave us a jar lid that we filled with water.

"What can we feed it?" we asked our mother.

She searched about until she found an eye dropper. Then she warmed some milk. Bob and I took turns trying to drip drops of milk into the bunny's mouth. We put the box near the range in the kitchen, the warmest place in the house.

When we got up the next morning, we ran to check on the rabbit. It was on its side. It didn't move. As we crouched down, an eye stared up at us.

On the snowy field, I stood still as Bob raised the rifle. *Boom!* The sound reverberated in my ears, echoing out through the still air. I looked ahead. There was a rabbit, lifeless, eyes open, bright blood spilling onto the pristine snow.

"I want to go home," I said.

"Well, then take the rabbit with you."

I didn't speak, didn't hold out my hand, but turned and, following our footprints, found my way back.

When I was older, in an attempt to be recognized, I began, as a 4-H project, to care for a calf that would be entered in the county fair. I found nothing appealing about grooming this animal who balked at my efforts and showed no acknowledgment of who I was, no appreciation of my hard work. Of course, my understanding that the second trip for the animal—following the first, to the fair—would be a lot less festive, made the job even less appealing. Why do all this to make the calf pretty, when the next trip the poor thing would take would be straight to the slaughterhouse? My project was short lived.

I gained a bit of independence when I obtained my driver's permit and took the job at the drive-in movie theater. A year later, with a license, I could pick up my friends and drive to Ortonville. My minimal paycheck allowed me to buy gas and oil for our aging Ford. My friend Flo would lean over me and through the open window instruct the attendant, "A dollar's worth of gas, and please fill it up with oil," as she handed me a few coins, her share of the cost.

My duties also branched out. My role during harvesting season had always revolved around helping my mother prepare food. Once I could drive, I began to deliver the lunches to the men and boys working in the fields.

Early in the day, my father gave me directions to the field where they'd be working. With the windows open and the sounds of nature as my companion, I drove down narrow dirt roads, often discovering areas new to me. When I reached my destination, I'd turn off the road slowly and carefully drive down the decline, then on up the other side of the ditch, where I'd park at the edge of the field. I'd honk the horn; the men would look up, cut all the engines, hurry to meet me and reach out for the drinks and sandwiches. Unspoken gratitude hung in the air.

One May morning, my father complained that there were not enough hands to prepare a field for planting. I volunteered to disc it.

"Are you sure you can do that?" he asked me.

Knowing that I'd be working on a plain expanse of dirt, with no plants to worry about driving over, I insisted that I was up to the job. However, I wasn't prepared for the dirt and dust that the wind whipped up as the hard ground was broken. It was a miserable job. When I finished and returned home, I couldn't jump off the Big Rock into the river to get clean, because the water was too cold. I took a long, long bath, shampooing my hair more than once, working hard to get all the dirt out. But the dirt was within me. That evening when I coughed and blew my nose, reminders of my day were visible on my handkerchief. I never volunteered for field work again.

But there came a time when Bob and I were told to harvest a field of flax. He was sixteen and I was fourteen. My father and mother had made plans to take a four-day trip with my aunt and uncle. For pleasure. This was a first for them.

Endless rain had delayed the harvesting.

Before my parents headed out, my father told Bob, "When the sun does come out, I want you and Barbara to get that last field west of town harvested."

On the day of their return, the sun *was* shining. So, early that morning, Bob started up the tractor and drove to the field. I followed in the truck. Right away, we found that the machine that bound the cut grain didn't work. The bale was hung up on the tying device. Bob stopped, telling me to take his place on the tractor seat. He hopped down and began to repair it.

Now, because no one could hear over the roar of the tractor's engine, signals had been devised. My brothers knew them well. A fast, circular hand motion meant the driver should release the clutch quickly. A slower motion meant release it slowly. I didn't know there was a second signal. Bob had signaled to let the clutch out slowly, very slowly, but I released it abruptly. With that, the steel kick-out bar spun rapidly, smashing Bob on the head.

I drove him home, where he lay down on the couch, passing in and out of consciousness. That's where my parents found him when they got back a few hours later. During the two days Bob was hospitalized, I was wracked with anxiety over how I had almost killed my brother.

In 2016, as he was retelling the story to me over the phone, I was grateful to learn that Bob, who still wears a scar from that day, bears no rancor toward me. I could hear the smile in his voice as he said, "We should've taught you those signals."

IV. MOTHER'S TURN

"I'd take a walk around the barn."
—Myrtle, when asked how
she managed to keep going

MEN TOLD THE STORIES

⌒

When a thunderstorm hit and my father and brothers were driven from the fields, they'd hurry to the house. They shook water and bits of straw off their jackets in the small shed before they entered the kitchen. They came in to wait it out until the sky cleared. When the temperatures dipped way down and the snow blew, they'd prop the shovels against the side of the house and come in, trailing drafts of frigid air behind. My father and brothers, and perhaps a neighbor who was lending a hand, would collapse on chairs around the table. As they waited, they talked of weather and market prices, a sick cow or a tractor that had to be repaired. My mother or one of my sisters or I would spoon coffee into the percolator, place cookies or slices of a cake on a plate, pour lemonade or milk, and coffee, always coffee. The men would acknowledge our offerings with a nod of the head, without breaking the rhythm of their words.

Men worked hard and became dirty, sweaty, and—always—hungry. They came into the house with slumped shoulders when the crops weren't doing well. They talked, but dispiritedly. Sometimes, but never consistently, when it seemed as though there might be a bumper crop, they stood taller and their voices boomed, making the rooms in our small house seem even smaller.

Contemporary scientists proclaim that people are no longer on top of the food chain. But on our farm, in our family, certain people were definitely at the top. My father raised cattle and pigs to be eaten. Chickens, too. And when he and my brothers hunted, it was as much for food as it was for sport.

And in our dwelling there was absolutely no doubt who was on top of that chain.

Sunday dinner was served an hour or so after we returned from Mass. Mother went from church to car to kitchen. I remember her trying to stall my siblings and me when we were clamoring for food. We had been fasting since the evening before.

"Just let me get my hat off," she'd say, as she did just that. Then she'd tie an apron over her Sunday dress and begin.

For the main meal of that special day, much of it partially prepared the previous evening, Mother often roasted a chicken—a succulent, very free-range, custom-raised chicken—that she'd chased, caught, and slaughtered the day before.

After removing the bird from the oven, she carved it and placed the pieces on a platter. One of us sisters carried the dish to the dining room and presented it to my father. After my mother slipped into her chair, together we said a hurried grace. Only then would my father begin by helping himself to one-half of the breast. He then handed the platter to my eldest brother, John, who took the second half of the breast. He passed the dish to Bill, my middle brother. Bill and Bob, the youngest boy, each took a thigh. The platter made its way around the table to Patt. She helped herself to the gizzard, which was considered the prize of the remaining pieces. Mother, with typical generosity, took the almost meatless neck, leaving the back of the bird for Helen. I waited as the wings, lonely on the platter, made their way to me.

The summer I turned fourteen, my mother traveled to St. Louis for two weeks to help my sister Patt when her first child was born. She left me in charge of feeding the men. I somehow persuaded Flo, a classmate, to help me. Of course, I'd been a part of the food routine my entire life, but those two weeks were a revelation. From 5:00 a.m. to 10:00 p.m., Flo and I were always doing something that involved food. Breakfast at 5:30 a.m.; a light lunch of sandwiches and cookies, packed and carried to the field at 10:00 a.m.; a full meat-potatoes-vegetables dinner at 12:00 p.m.; a lunch—again in the field—of sandwiches and cookies at 3:00 p.m.; a hearty supper at 6:00 p.m; and the last food of the day: cake or cookies, or perhaps ice cream with strawberries from the garden, at 9:30 p.m.

My father and brothers talked as Flo and I served. She and I fried and baked, peeled and mashed, mixed and stirred. And we washed and washed dishes and pans. By hand, of course.

After the harvest, their talk turned to hunting. The basics. What, where, and with whom were cause for lively debates. Walking through tall grasses during pheasant season, my father and brothers would be quiet, but in winter when the ice on the lake was frozen hard they'd retreat to a fish house where, in self-imposed exile, there was plenty of time to talk. I assume that the words flowed.

The usual rhythm of our household was broken for a few days each year when my two great-uncles, Hank and Bill, traveled from an area of Montana that was still frontier-like at that time, to Big Stone City, which to them was an oasis of civilization. They were like Mutt and Jeff, one tall and large, with a huge belly (that was Bill), the other short and slight (Hank). My mother invited them to join us for Sunday dinners.

While my mother hurried to finish the meal, the three generations of men gathered in our living room. My brothers and, for the most part, my father were quiet and listened, as Hank and Bill told nonstop stories of their adventures. While I helped my mother by setting the table, I was aware of the words coming faster and faster and the voices growing louder, until, after a short pause, there'd be whoops of thigh-slapping laughter. I knew I wasn't welcome in that room. No female would have been. The storytelling continued while my mother stirred the gravy one more time.

When we all sat down at the table, my mother was mostly silent. If she spoke, it was only to ask if someone wanted more mashed potatoes or another cup of coffee.

Now here, so many years later, are a few of the stories my mother never had a chance to tell during those times, but which she passed on to me. I've used my knowledge of the times, places, and people to re-create the events she described.

FIRST DRIVE OUT

⌒

1926

It was during May, as a fiancée, that my mother made the trek from the city to the farm to meet her future in-laws. Sitting beside Roy, my father, in the black Model T borrowed from his father for the trek, she would have been alert as the seemingly endless miles of flat, treeless prairie shifted to a terrain of gently rolling hills, streams, and an occasional lake. As trees became more numerous, she would have noted the new leaves on the cottonwoods, thriving along the banks of streams and small lakes, their newly unfurled leaves now, for a short-lived time, an indescribable mix of yellow and green.

For the first hour or so of the trip, they'd discussed the date of the wedding and their plans for a honeymoon in the Black Hills, but as they continued east, the sameness of the dips and rises lulled them into a relaxed silence. Myrtle had time to contemplate her—no, their—new life together.

What will Roy's parents be like? she may have wondered. Roy had told her enough about his father that she believed he would welcome her, but she wasn't so sure about her mother-in-law-to-be. She hoped that what she was taking to give them was sufficient. She'd asked her sister Marian for advice.

"I think it should be something I've made. But nothing baked. Roy told me his mother is a fine baker, and I don't want to compete with her."

Marian had been quiet for a while. "What if I make my divinity? If we pack it carefully, it'll arrive in perfect condition."

So, the previous evening, while Myrtle packed, Marian had measured and stirred.

"Tell me when it starts to set," Myrtle had called from the bedroom. "I want to be able to say I made it."

"Of course," Marian had called back with a laugh.

And so began a tradition: making the cloud-like candy, packing it carefully, and transporting it from Pierre to the farmhouse. For almost fifty years, Marian always arrived, after making the long drive, suitcase in one hand and a box of divinity in the other.

Roy and Myrtle had ridden in silence for quite some time when he slowed and swung over to a small store, where he bought gasoline. Shortly after that, he turned north, onto a smaller road.

"We're at the edge of the Coteau des Prairies at this point," he said. "The highest elevation in the eastern part of the state."

The ascent had been so gradual, Myrtle had been unaware they'd been climbing, but when she looked out, she saw below her a sea of green stretching out for miles into the distance.

Myrtle sat up a little taller and watched the passing scenery attentively. A few hours later, Roy slowed the car, shifted down, and turned right onto a narrow dirt road.

THREE DAYS IN JUNE

⌒

The first pangs of labor began June 25, 1927, late that Friday morning. Myrtle was alone in the house. Roy was out cutting hay in the South Field, taking advantage of the sunny day. She really had no choice but to wait until he returned to tell him the news. When she heard him stomp his feet outside the side door in an effort to shake off loose bits of leaves and dirt, she was relieved. She hadn't timed her contractions, but she was aware that they had become more frequent. When he entered, the spicy smell of freshly cut alfalfa came with him. She was grateful for that. For the past few weeks, barn odors had made her gag.

Myrtle set bowls of potatoes and vegetables and a platter of pork chops on the table and sat down. When Roy noticed that she hadn't taken a bite, he looked at her closely. That's when she told him. He pushed back the chair and stood up, still chewing as he did so.

"I'll harness up," he said.

"You can finish your meal."

"No, no. I'll be back in just a minute."

My parents weren't nervous about this first birth. My mother's pregnancy had been uneventful, and the midwife's reputation was positive. More important, they knew her and her assistant well; the two women were my father's maiden aunts, Ella and Mary. Years earlier, Ella had journeyed to Minneapolis, where she'd received formal nursing training.

And so it was on a beautiful spring day that my father helped my mother into the buggy and together they rode up the hill and along the dirt road. Should he allow the horse to go as fast as safely possible? Or slow the mare down before they approached each rut? As a result, his signals to the horse were confusing. In the end, he gave her full rein, but he pulled her in as they approached a major road of South Dakota that served as Big Stone's main street. People waved in greeting to my parents, but, uncharacteristically, my father didn't follow suit. My mother didn't even notice the greetings. Once past the brickworks and the canning factory, he urged the horse forward. They crossed the state line into Minnesota.

"Giddyap!" he shouted, jiggling the reins and then letting them hang loose.

When they reached the Ortonville town limits, he pulled the mare into a walk. Just before the courthouse, he guided her right and up the steep incline. He pulled over in front of a two-story white frame house.

"Please stay here," my father said, as he jumped down from the buggy. He hurried up the steps and banged on the front door. Ella and Mary were there almost immediately. My father didn't have to say a word. The two women glanced toward the buggy and then quickly followed him to the wagon, where they helped my mother down.

My father had done his part. He was no longer needed.

"We'll call the Big Stone operator when we have news for you," Ella said.

My father managed to kiss my mother on the top of her head before the two women firmly closed the door.

My mother once told me how these two kind spinsters viewed pregnancy. To them, it was disgraceful because it was a visible acknowledgment of the activities that had precipitated it. It was not to be recognized and *certainly* not to be discussed.

"But when the babies came, they just loved those little ones!" she said.

By the tone of her voice, I knew she was completely mystified at the aunts' inexplicable disregard for the principles of logic.

So my father left the white house and retreated to Big Stone—to the familiarity of the little café that sat across the street from the telephone office, and to the comfort of longtime friends and acquaintances. Late in the afternoon, with no word yet, he drove the buggy to his father's farm, fourteen miles west of town. There, he talked to my grandfather and the two of them agreed: My father's youngest brother, Earl, would stay at my father's farm so he could feed and milk the cows. In that way, my father would be free to wait for the news and respond.

That evening, my father returned to the white house on the hill. Again he knocked.

"Not much progress," Ella reported, as she opened the door.

She gave no more information. My father waited in the parlor, falling in and out of sleep. He continued to wait through the entire next day. In the meantime, my aunts were praying and employing all of the wisdom they possessed.

Late Sunday evening, my father had again dozed off, so he wasn't aware when Mary slipped out the back of the house, ran two doors to the neighbor who had a telephone, and, in desperation, called the doctor. This doctor, the only one in Big Stone City or Ortonville, was known to enjoy alcohol way too much for one in his profession. My father awoke when, an hour or so later, Mary ushered the doctor in. My father stood up to greet him, but the doctor didn't stop as he followed Mary to the back bedroom.

Now my father was alert and on his feet. Time dragged. When he heard the first cry, he slumped back on the couch, relieved and drained of all energy. Because of that, he didn't act fast enough to detain the doctor as he left. He heard only a few gruff words—"Mother and baby fine"—before the door closed.

Now he was impatient to see my mother, but his aunts were obsessive about cleanliness and appearance, and he knew there'd be another wait.

When Ella did enter the room, she announced, "A baby girl." She wasn't smiling.

"Myrtle is fine, Roy. But things didn't go as planned. With the doctor. The baby's not quite right." She struggled to complete her report. "She can't suck. Don't worry. We'll find a way to feed . . . What have you named her?"

My father looked down.

"Dorothy."

Dorothy. Firstborn. First paternal grandchild. First maternal grandchild.

Hopes, expectations, dreams, all crushed forever by metal forceps. Delicate bones broken before the baby cried for the first time.

Dorothy. The firstborn, who never learned to sit, crawl, walk, speak. Somehow my mother cared for her, kept her alive. Somehow, through nights and days without sleep (my mother told me she sometimes fell asleep while standing), she nurtured and loved her.

She spoke to me of the tragic event only one time. Her voice was very soft, and I had to move closer to hear her words.

"When the doctor was leaning over me, I smelled liquor on his breath."

"Oh, Mother," I said. "I'm so sorry."

A CUP OF TEA

◥

Myrtle was stirring the white clothes, trying to keep her large belly from touching the hot iron range, when she heard Blackie's warning bark. The dog was harmless, but he felt it his job to announce the presence of strangers, and the low, resonating growl from his throat as people came forward made them hesitate before they drew near.

Myrtle leaned the wooden pole that she'd been using against the side of the boiler and wiped her hands on her apron. She was perplexed. Annoyed. No one came calling on a Monday afternoon. She certainly didn't have time to visit.

Today the wind had stopped blowing, and she had to get two weeks of laundry done in one day. There was no way of drying clothes when the wind blew. Dust was everywhere. Outside in piles and drifts. Inside the house, on the windowsills, on the floor, in dresser drawers and kitchen cupboards. In a person's mouth, eyes, ears, bowels.

Even in Myrtle's dreams. When she awoke some mornings, her eyelids felt heavy as she opened them, and there was dust on her pillow. One day it had blown so hard and so black that she was worried the children might get lost on their way home from school. Roy had driven to town to pick them up.

How had she gotten to this? As a young woman, she'd yearned to be a mother. Her own mother had died when she was small. After that, there'd been little laughter when her two stern aunts had moved into their house. As the oldest, Myrtle soon became a source of comfort for her sisters and brother. So when Roy had proposed to her on that now seemingly distant day, she'd been eager to begin a family of her own.

And this afternoon she had time to work without interruption. Dorothy was quiet in her crib. John was with Roy, who was trying to divert water from the river to the South Field. Patt and Helen had asked if they could go see if there was any young fruit on the wild plum tree out in the pasture.

Myrtle realized that she should have told them to stay and help her. There had been a dull, unending pain in her lower back Saturday, Sunday, and now today also.

She'd let them go, thinking the girls had so little fun in their young lives. Myrtle sensed they were anxious. The garden would probably produce nothing this summer but some small knobs of potatoes.

Myrtle had stopped hoping for rain, though she still prayed for it. Everyone did, even those who didn't go to church. At this point, her hope rested on the wind. Each morning she woke hoping that the wind wouldn't blow that day, and some days— today was one—it didn't.

Blackie's growl turned to yelping. Could she invite a visitor into her house? The room was hot and humid, and the air was sharp with the smell of Hylex, which didn't mask the ammonia smell of diapers.

There was a light rap on the screen door, and Myrtle hurriedly brushed her hair back from her face. She walked through the kitchen and by a pile of light-colored clothes into the entryway, where the dark work clothes lay in a huge, collapsing mound.

An old man with a scruffy beard and a grimy face looked back at her through the mesh of the screen door.

Should she let him in? She was vulnerable, but she could never turn someone away who needed help.

"Good afternoon."

"Yes?"

"I'm sorry to disturb you."

"How can I help you?"

"I was wondering, could you . . . Could you make me a cup of tea?"

Myrtle hesitated. You never let anyone stand on the step. You always invited a visitor in, even salesmen when you had no money to buy their goods.

"We're coffee drinkers in this family. But maybe I have some tea in the back of the cupboard. I'll look."

"Thanks. That's kind of you."

"If you'd like to wash up, there's water in that covered barrel, and then, if you'd like to come in . . ."

"I would like to wash up."

Myrtle was aware of the way the man said "wash." She knew he wasn't from here. The way he said the word was a reminder of the sounds of the friends and family she'd left behind. When she'd come to this part of South Dakota as a bride, she'd noticed that people said the word differently here. They said "warsh," not "wash," and the mispronunciation irritated her.

She knew exactly where she lived now. Anyone could put his finger instantly on the Hoffbecks' piece of earth on the map. Just below the curve of a quarter moon, cut out of northeastern South Dakota from its neighboring state by two long, narrow lakes.

Where was this man from?

"Would you like to come in?"

"No, no. I don't want to be any bother."

Myrtle recalled a story her family told about her mother, Theresa. Myrtle remembered her only a little. She died when Myrtle was five.

In another hard period of history, Theresa fed the hoboes who stopped by her kitchen door. She always insisted that they eat a complete meal: meat, potatoes, a vegetable, even homemade pickles. When they'd finished that, she gave them a cup of coffee and a piece of pie.

Her mother commented once how there seemed to be more and more hoboes each year. No one told her, though perhaps she knew all along, that the hoboes had carved the rough shape of a kettle in the bark near the base of the old elm in her front yard—a sign to all of them that a generous, gracious lady lived there.

"Are you sure you won't come in?"

"No, I'm just fine out here on the step with this friendly dog of yours. Thank you, ma'am."

"Ma'am?" She hated being called ma'am. It made her feel old. Did she look old? Myrtle thought of herself as she appeared in the photograph taken in her father's yard the afternoon of her wedding. Smooth skin, wide-open eyes, a smile just beginning.

The photo had been on the dresser all those years. Until the dust started blowing. Then she'd taken it, wrapped it in brown paper, and placed it in the cedar chest. Myrtle wondered if the dust was finding its way into the cedar chest. Was the photo aging as fast as she was?

She put a kettle of water on the range and opened the top cupboard door. There was a small, dusty package of tea way in the back, and when she saw it she remembered that Aunt Mary had given it to her when Bill, her youngest son, had been so ill. She reached high and took the teapot down from the top shelf, wiped off the outside, and rinsed it out with a little of the water that was heating.

Myrtle walked back to the door, picking up an old towel from a cabinet knob as she went. She opened the door.

"Here, you can dry with this."

He raised his face. With a start Myrtle realized the man was not old. His eyes were sky blue, and his face was unlined, except for little creases. He was a good-looking man with a broad forehead.

Why had this young man left his family? Where was he from?

"How did you happen to come here?"

"I was riding the train. I'm on my way to the Twin Cities."

Myrtle had read about men who rode the freight cars, trying to find a place, any place, where there was work. He would have come from the west, passed through Pierre. She had been back only once in the twelve years since her wedding. Her father had been ill. It must have been seven years now since she had sat beneath the elm with its swing of her childhood, walked her girlhood streets.

"And," the young man was continuing, "I saw this line of green winding out in front of me. It was the first green I'd seen in days. When the train slowed, I jumped off." He sounded rather proud of himself. "I just followed the green."

"That would be the weeds in our riverbed. It's almost dry now." *If this drought continues forever*, Myrtle wondered, *and we're at last blown away, will there still be that line of green?*

"Could I fix you a sandwich?"

"No. Thank you."

"I have some meat left over from our dinner."

"No. I couldn't let you do that. I see that you have a lot of mouths to feed each meal."

He glanced at the pile of laundry beside her and—did she only imagine it?—down at her belly.

Myrtle blushed. "I'll get your tea, then."

She returned with the cup of tea, opened the screen door, and handed it to him.

"Thank you. I'll just sit here, if you don't mind."

"That's fine."

Myrtle returned to her work. Where had her life led her that a stranger felt that she could not afford to give him a sandwich? The piles on the floor seemed to press in on her; the odors and the heavy air brought a sour taste to her mouth. Her movements were awkward as she took the stick, pulled the clothes from the steaming water, and dropped them into a tin basin.

More and more lately, she felt as though her endless work was burying her. Dorothy would always be in diapers. Now, soon, there would be another in diapers, also. Would her life always be some mad story of alternating chapters of one in diapers, two in diapers?

Although there were no sounds from the step, Myrtle was aware of the young man. It was true they had no money, but neither did any of their neighbors. This was a bad time for everyone they knew. But they did manage to eat, and they had their beds each night. When had the young man last eaten a good meal? Where would he sleep tonight?

She slipped out to the porch and from there down to the cellar, where she stored leftovers in a wooden chest with ice. She saw the remainder of a beef roast, some cut-up cooked potatoes, milk in a covered jar, and eggs she had hard-boiled to keep them from spoiling. Somehow, looking at the food made her feel better.

Back upstairs, she picked up the teapot and went to the door.

"Would you like some more tea?"

"If it's no bother."

"We won't be drinking it."

She filled his cup.

"Do you see our chickens?"

"Yes."

"Well, as long as there are weeds and their seeds, the chickens will have something to eat."

"Yes, I suppose." His voice sounded puzzled, as though he thought she'd gone a little strange.

Myrtle left him drinking his tea then and moved back into the kitchen.

A few minutes later, she returned and handed him a small package wrapped in newspaper.

"What's this?"

"Hard-cooked eggs. Two for your supper and two for your breakfast."

"Uh, no . . ."

She looked at the young man with a steady gaze. She knew that she'd remember him for the rest of her life.

"Please take them. We'll always have weeds, you see."

The creases by his eyes deepened, and a smile touched his mouth.

"Ah, yes. Thank you."

"My pleasure," she said, and then turned back to her work.

MIDNIGHT COMPANIONS

Myrtle's eyes close; her head falls forward, then snaps up with a jerk. She must stay awake to watch the river. She stands, goes to the window, and looks out. The moon and stars give enough light that she can see the pool of water fifteen yards down the slope. The gravel path leads not to the gate to the feed pasture, but to dark water where dirty, snow-covered chunks of ice float and bob in a new and widening pool. Myrtle pulls Roy's work jacket off a hook near the kitchen door, pushes her feet, shoes and all, into some old work boots, and steps out into the night.

The smell of wet earth floats to her face. She takes in a breath. She has always welcomed this smell, the first hint, sometimes as early as January during a short thaw, that there will be another spring. The promise that, for a few short months, there will be no stove to feed and tend, ashes to carry out, frozen clothes to take from the line, stiff, body-like shapes that remain rough to the skin even when completely dry and ironed. The end, for a time, of horrible colds, of handkerchiefs, heavy with mucus, and sometimes blood, to be soaked and bleached and washed and dried and ironed, ugly daytime mementos of nights up with fretful children, on and on, week after week.

Blackie comes out of the shadows near the step and nudges her leg nervously. Myrtle runs her hand over his silky head. "Don't worry, we won't forget you."

It has been a hard winter. Well, what winter isn't hard? Her lips move slightly up at the corners. Not as cold as some, but more snow than in seven years. All winter, it has seemed that as soon as Roy and John shovel the paths—from the house to the barn, from the barn to the hog shed—and then open up the road to the town, the white flakes begin to fall again, covering their work, making each time clearing the paths harder, as the banks of shoveled snow grow above their heads. Now, it has turned too warm too quickly and the river is rising.

They are as ready for the water as they can be. Helen and Patt have moved the baby chicks from the brooder house, the building closest to the water, to the upstairs hall in the house. The cows and hogs will be safe in the barn and shed. Those buildings are on a small hill. Before Roy went to bed, exhausted from filling and stacking gunny sacks of gravel, he and Myrtle agreed: if the water reaches the lowest limb of the basswood tree, she will wake him, and then they will wake the children. Roy has parked the car about a quarter of a mile away, on top of the Big Hill. The mud makes it impossible to use the driveway. The children will walk, each carrying a box—a change of clothes for everyone, Myrtle's wedding china and silver, a few photos, the crucifix that had rested on her mother's coffin.

Dorothy is too heavy to be carried that far, so John has brought the long sled from the barn. He will pull her over the mud. The sled stands ready, propped by the kitchen door. It worries Myrtle that Dorothy may be afraid. She hasn't been out of the house for the last ten of her fourteen years. The children will help her, though. They seem to be able to make a game out of almost any event. This afternoon, while Myrtle spread newspapers and wondered if she will ever be able to get the chicken smell out of the house, Bob and Barbara made fences and barricades for the baby chicks from old magazines. Shortly after that, Roy ordered Bob to walk with Barbara to their grandparents' house in town. Both of them are safe there now.

A distant crack. An ice cake toppling a tree farther upstream. *Hoo-ha, hoo-ha.* An owl's call. Myrtle pulls the jacket close around her and reaches down to Blackie. She remembers the first time she came to this place. Roy brought her to see their future home a few months before the wedding. It was spring. The trees wore little wisps of yellow and green leaves. Robins hopped on tufts of new grass. The fragrance of lilac blossoms was intense, distilled and concentrated, held from wandering by the hills that encircled the small farm. The river murmured and gurgled. The beauty, the promise, of her new life made her eager to begin. How innocent she was. She planned long walks in the woods and over the nearby prairie, looking for wildflowers unknown to her. She dreamed of spreading a shawl, leaning back on soft grass in the sun's warm breath. Myrtle imagined their new life, their unborn children, fresh and perfect as that spring day. Those feelings are remote now, so deeply buried after Dorothy's birth that it is hard for Myrtle to retrieve even a shadow of them.

Oh my God, dear God, did you have this planned all along? Or if it was not planned, because there is free will, after all, then did you know that this was what was to be? Dear Lord, I'm so tired. So lonely. I haven't even thought that before. No time to realize I'm lonely! Is that part of Your plan, then? Keep me so busy, so tired, that I can't even feel? Just keep me moving and working another day? It isn't just people or visiting I need; it's relief, some hope that things will get better. Last spring when I saw the new Easter hats in church, I didn't envy the ribbons or flowers—I resented the promise of renewal those hats represented.

Myrtle remembers a Saturday afternoon the spring of her senior year. Just for fun, she and her sisters set out to try on every new hat in Pierre. In the first store, they managed to appear serious, carefully modeling one hat and then another, solemnly deciding against each one. But in the second store, when Marian tried on an outrageous scarlet cloche with ostrich feathers, all of them began to giggle. They ran out of the store and around the corner. As Myrtle remembers the color of that hat, the sound of her sisters' laughter echoing off nearby buildings, the softness of their bodies as they held each other, her days and this night close in on her, drab and empty.

Myrtle looks up at the sky. The moon is no longer visible, but its reflected light makes a soft glow in the east beyond the hills. The sky is magnificent and humbling. Myrtle walks to the step, picks up the long sled, and carries it to a flat, open space in the middle of the yard. She sits on it, then lies back, resting her head on her hands, face to the sky.

At a grand and glorious distance, the Milky Way sweeps across the sky, the stars as individual and numerous as grains of powdered sugar on the surface of a chocolate cake. Lower, much closer—if she took the tall ladder from the barn, she thinks, she could reach up and touch them—are the diamonds of the Big Dipper, and there, nearer yet, the Little Dipper. Myrtle sees movement out of the corner of her eye and turns her head. A star falls gently, lightly, and then, before it disappears, she sees another fall near the first, and then yet another. Myrtle watches closely, hoping the shower of falling stars will continue. Blackie brushes her face with his nose and woofs anxiously. Myrtle puts her arm around his neck and pulls him close.

"It'll be all right," she whispers into his soft neck.

His rough tongue wipes her face. Myrtle holds the dog close for a moment and then gets up to go check on the river.

THE EMPTY CRIB

Before Myrtle opens her eyes, raises her head from the pillow, before she realizes it is midafternoon, not early morning, she feels a pain clamping down, deep in her middle. Something—for one horrible thump of her heart, she can't remember what—is different. Something is terribly wrong.

Dorothy. Dorothy is gone. With an effort of will, she sits up, leans down, and puts on her shoes. She stands. Then, leaving the bed in disarray, she walks to the dining room, to the corner where the large, varnished oak crib stands empty. A worn blanket lies at its end. A small pillow with an indentation rests at its head. The clock on the buffet sounds a steady *tock-tock, tock-tock*. Myrtle picks up the blanket. It was once a deep rose color. After being washed every Monday for so many years, it has lost its beauty. It is now the color of flesh. Myrtle holds the blanket close against her chest, then folds it neatly into a rectangle and replaces it at the foot of the crib. She doesn't pick up the pillow to fluff it, but instead leaves it with its head-shaped hollow.

At that meeting in the rectory last spring with Roy and Father Esterguard, she'd asked that Dorothy not be moved until fall, to allow her daughter to enjoy one more summer, with its gentle breezes moving the white curtains at the window, one more summer hearing the noise and laughter of her brothers and sisters. It seemed a small victory for Myrtle and a big one for Dorothy.

But today she knows that she miscalculated. On that cool May evening when she let her hold on Dorothy slip, she didn't think ahead to realize that this fall Barbara will start school. Myrtle realizes she is alone in the house for the first time since Dorothy's birth, seventeen years ago. And the emptiness of the house taunts her.

Father Esterguard began by saying, "Dorothy's getting too much for you," but stopped when Myrtle shook her head and looked at him.

"Uh . . ." He paused, then began again. "You must think not just of Dorothy, but of your other children as well." He cleared his throat. "Helen and Patt are teenagers now. They need to be able to bring their friends home without . . ." He stopped, started again. "Without . . ." He swallowed.

Myrtle noticed his Adam's apple disappearing below his Roman collar, then reappearing. She did not look directly at Roy but knew he was staring at his hands, where he was flipping his jackknife over and over. It reminded Myrtle of a fish she had seen caught in a pool of the shrinking river one recent summer.

"Without," Myrtle finished the priest's sentence, looking at him with steady eyes, "being embarrassed."

His silence let her know that she was correct.

She remembered the time two years earlier when Patt and Helen had run to her, both angry and talking over each other.

A classmate had visited our house for the first time. The girl had entered the dining room and, upon seeing the crib in the corner, walked right up to it and peered inside.

"What is that?" she'd asked, with scorn in her voice. She pointed and began to laugh.

Myrtle had been unable to find words to ease Patt and Helen's pain.

At that meeting with Father Esterguard, she'd agreed that Dorothy be moved to the hospital to be taken care of by the sisters, as the two men had suggested, though not immediately, but rather in a few months, in early September. They'd quickly granted her that request, grateful, she knew, that she'd neither argued nor cried. This morning as she worked, she'd been able to avoid thinking, able to ignore the pain of her betrayal, but at their midday dinner, after grace, as Roy ate and listened intently, with furrowed brow, to the radio, the time when she had always fed Dorothy, her pain became physical and she was unable to eat. What was Dorothy thinking now? She must be asking, *Where is my mother? Why did she leave me here? When will she come back for me?* Myrtle sat still. Then after the rapid, excited reporting of the cattle and hog futures ended and the Folgers commercial began, Roy turned down the radio and looked at her questioningly.

Myrtle spoke: "Who's feeding her now?"

He didn't ask whom she was inquiring about. "The sisters, of course."

"They'll hurry her. She'll gag."

"The sisters will know how to do it. They'll understand."

"She's only used to me. She'll be so scared. Maybe she won't be able to eat at all."

Roy stopped. Myrtle knew he was frustrated, knowing there was nothing he could say that would help. He was quiet as he continued to eat, the sound of his fork and knife hitting the plate echoing in the small room. Myrtle got up to serve coffee, poured a cup for Roy, and stayed standing. She certainly couldn't drink any coffee, but, to be polite, she sat again.

When Roy finished his coffee, he got up and came to stand behind her chair. Resting his hands on her shoulders, he pulled her back gently so that her head rested on his chest. Then he leaned down and kissed the top of her head.

THE WHITE DRESS

M y sister Helen made the dress Dorothy wore to heaven. Taking an old dress of Dorothy's, she opened up all the seams and used the pieces as a pattern. After supper, while I was helping Mother wash the dishes, she took the tablecloth and the protective pads off the dining room table and laid out the shining cotton that she had bought at Penney's in Ortonville.

All that evening, she cut and pressed and sewed. By morning, only the hem was left to be done. The sleeves were long, with three pearl buttons on each cuff. The small, round collar was trimmed with white lace, and, down the front, rows of more flowery lace made a tiny garden of white.

Helen made a long sash. Bob and I stood there, watching her push the needle in and out. Bob asked her why she worked so hard to make the edges perfect. No one would see the sash, anyway.

Helen stopped sewing and very slowly put the needle with the thread still attached to it under a few strands on the spool. She didn't answer Bob, didn't even look at him. She stood and tenderly smoothed the folds of the dress. She then held out each end of the sash away from her to make sure they matched perfectly.

V. WE BEGIN TO LEAVE

ONE BY ONE

⌐—⌐

When I envision those years on the farm, I think of us all
together—squabbling, working, laughing—but in reality
there wasn't much time when we were all there, sleeping alone
or, more likely, sharing a bed, under the shingled roof of our
farmhouse.

When Helen was four, she was sent to live with our father's
parents, Bert and Anna, on their farm northwest of Big Stone.
That farm, unlike ours, wasn't set near a river in the woods but
rather sat exposed on the open prairie. The only trees were Russian olives, planted in rows at the edges of fields in an attempt to
tame the unending winds. Not that many years earlier, the land
had been plowed for the first time, by my grandfather. He'd filed
the necessary government papers to establish it as homestead
property for his sister.

The teacher of the one-room schoolhouse boarded with
Bert and Anna. When the teacher walked the mile to school, she
took Helen with her. For two years, she helped Helen learn as
she taught her older pupils. Helen returned to our farm in time
to enroll in first grade in the town elementary school.

Bill, who almost died from an allergic reaction to the smallpox vaccination he received at six months and who, as a toddler,

was often in agony because of his severe, chronic eczema, needed extra care, so he, too, was sent to live with Bert and Anna. He continued to live with them when they moved to town. Bill rejoined our family when he was ten; by that age, he could lend substantial help with the chores.

Both Helen and Bill basked in the attention of Bert and Anna, who were strict but loving grandparents. As far as long-term effects of this time away went, their reactions are evidence of what we already know: siblings view things differently from their earliest days. For Helen, it was a positive experience.

"I loved my teacher in that little school. I was doing so well, but when I began school in town, I floundered. It set me back, I never recovered academically."

Bill concurs—"I never could catch up with my classmates in town"—but blames the one-room schoolhouse, calling it a "disservice."

Both of these drastic actions were taken to give relief to my mother. During those years, she had not only an infant and a tod-dler to care for, but Dorothy as well. And because Dorothy didn't have control over her muscles, she couldn't cooperate in the dia-per-changing or bathing process. My mother was working with dead weight. And, of course, Dorothy still needed to be spoon-fed.

It exhausts me to think of all those diapers that were added each time a new baby arrived. More diapers to be added to the sheets and dirty work clothes that, in a series of exhausting steps, had to be made wearable again. And there were the meals to be cooked, the dishes to be washed.

What space of time were we all together on the farm? I was born in 1939. Dorothy died in 1947. So there were only eight years when my siblings and I were all alive.

But that's not the number I'm trying to calculate. Bill knows he returned at some point during 1945, the year Dorothy was taken to live with the nuns. He isn't sure how old he was when he was sent to live with our grandparents, but it was certainly before he turned three. There are five years between Bill and me. As I ponder these numbers, I realize, with astonishment, there was never a time when we were all together in our farmhouse.

Our family continually expanded and contracted. It seems as though that shifting style was somewhat of a family tradition.

Only a year or so after they'd emigrated from Denmark to Minnesota, Bert, my grandfather, and his brother, Ness, both bachelors, welcomed an infant girl into their home. A neighbor woman had died in childbirth, and her husband, overcome with grief, suffered a nervous breakdown. He wasn't capable of caring for his baby daughter. Somehow those brothers, my grandfather and great-uncle—only in their early twenties—did just that, bringing the baby into their house, which was little more than a cabin, while they continued the hard work of cultivating the first crops on the new land.

And then, years later, after Bert had married, moved to South Dakota, and raised children of his own, he persuaded Anna that they should take in two elementary school-age neighbor girls after their parents had been killed in an automobile accident.

The separation from Helen and Bill must have been wrenching for my mother. But time and circumstance demanded that she be practical. She knew that Helen and Bill would receive more care and attention from their grandparents than she could give. Her understanding and flexibility had a limit, however.

My mother's brother, Brit, lived in Sioux Falls, a city 120 miles south of our farm. He was a civil engineer, a career that offered opportunity and good wages, even during those depression years. He and his wife, Anne, were economically secure, but they were unhappy. They wanted a child, and Anne was unable to become pregnant.

During one of their occasional visits to our farm, Anne and Brit waited until after my mother had stopped working, long after she'd made and served dinner, after Dorothy had been tended to and Helen and Patt tucked into their shared bed—waited, I imagine, until the moment when my father, in his nightly ritual, stepped out onto the porch to check the night sky. It was then that they looked at each other and with a nod agreed that it was the right time.

It would have been Brit who spoke first. He would have begun slowly, tentatively.

"Myrtle, we see that you have more than you can do. You're exhausted. We can help. We have resources and can give a child the best of everything. Would you please consider this? We'd like to have Patsy come live with us."

He hesitated, then added, "We'd like to adopt her."

At the time, Patt was three. Mother told him she'd have to discuss it with Roy. My father supported my mother, and together they told Brit and Anne, "No, we won't give up our daughter."

Patt stayed. But when she learned of this offer as a teenager, she wasn't grateful that she'd stayed with us but rather became resentful, imagining the easy life that could have been hers. A life that would have been rich in cultural activities, as well as material belongings. A life where she wouldn't have had to work so hard to earn her way through college. A life far removed from the unending toil demanded of all of us.

Of course, her resentment toward our father played a part in this, too. One summer afternoon when Patt was twelve, our father rushed into the house from the yard. Hummy, a mixed breed that Patt loved and considered *her* dog, had been chasing the chickens. Our father returned with the rifle, and, as Patt watched helplessly, he aimed and shot the dog dead. She never forgave him.

The last time I saw Patt, who died in 2009, heavy bitterness weighed down her frail voice when she spoke of that day our father killed Hummy.

When our parents were making those serious, painful decisions to send Helen and Bill away, to refuse the adoption offer, there was never a discussion about one presence. Dorothy stayed with us for eleven more years.

PACKING UP

Our family began to shrink. After she graduated from high school, Helen left for Minneapolis, where she enrolled in business school. She packed quietly and left without a fuss. The next year, there was more drama as Patt prepared to leave.

Patt's gone. Mother and I helped her get ready.

Yesterday we washed and starched her blouses and skirts. Patt and I hauled them out to the lawn in a large basket. She held one handle in her left hand; I held the other with both my hands, shuffling sideways down the south porch steps.

Patt likes to do everything in a hurry. Everything. I asked her once if she slept fast, too. She gave me one of her smiles. I knew what that meant. I'm nine years younger than she is. But then she stopped smiling and looked serious.

"I wish I could sleep faster, but no one can. I just sleep less. Just think of it. Use your math, Barb. One less hour of sleep a day, and in a week I've saved another person's working day. And if ever you can't sleep at night, don't just lie there! Turn on the light and read. Don't waste time trying to get back to sleep. There's so much to do."

For Patt, wasting time was a sin.

Yesterday my job was to pick up a piece of clothing, shake it out fast, and hold it up to her. She'd take it and quickly fasten it to the line with two wooden clothespins, using the last pin for the next piece, so the corners of two garments shared one pin.

Change was in the air. The wild asters in the low weeds at the edge of the lawn were still in bloom, but their vivid blue-purple was now pale and faded, the color of a dress washed over and over. Blackbirds in the trees seemed to be arguing about when to go south. They jabbered amid the branches, then burst into the air, flapping around before they regrouped. Were they looking for their brothers and sisters so they could make the trip together?

A cool breeze hinted at winter storms.

"Barb, next piece!" Patt kept at her chore. When she'd finished, the clothespins stood at attention all down the line. The wind billowed and filled the blouses and skirts, setting them to dancing.

Later, Patt and I went out again. The clothes were dry now and smelled a little of soap, a little of September sunshine. As we reversed the process, the blouses and skirts felt stiff. Patt tossed the clothes into the basket, the pins onto the grass. I picked up the pins and put them into their cloth bag.

The breeze was cooler, and the shadows of the tall trees beyond the lawn began to fold over the sunshine on the grass. It was quiet now. The blackbirds had flown away.

One day I asked Patt why she was going to college. She had a good job: checking out food in the Ortonville grocery store. When she was paid, she'd always buy us something. We have lettuce even in winter now; before that, it was only cabbage, picked from our garden and stored down in the cellar. Sometimes she brought home bananas or grapes, and once, close to Christmas, she brought a pineapple, saying it was all the way from Hawaii.

Another time, Patt carried a small brown bag with the top twisted tight. I thought it was candy. I took it from her, started to open it, but she stopped me. Then she pulled the top apart just a crack. When I looked in, I saw a horrible brown bug with skinny legs and long, thin feelers pointing at me. My stomach turned, and I tasted something icky in my mouth.

"That's a cockroach. They come in fruit crates. Always wash fruit before you eat it."

For a long time, I only ate apples from the trees in our garden.

When I asked Patt why she was going, she looked at me and said, "I have to go to college. When you're my age, you do, too. I must get through college. Then I'm going to do so much—pan for gold in Alaska, look for black diamonds in the Amazon, dig up old cities in the Arabian desert!"

When she talked like that, I believed her.

Back in the house, Patt sprinkled each blouse and each skirt with water, her hand flying above them in little jerks, spreading dark blotches where the droplets hit. Then she rolled the clothes up in neat logs so they would be just right for ironing.

Patt set up the board and began ironing while Mother folded. Patt was quiet. I missed her talking. She always told stories of what she'd heard in town. And Mother didn't hum her bits of opera, either. I could hear the clock ticking and tried to think of a question to ask, but this time I couldn't.

So it was quiet while Mother took each blouse, laid it front down on the table, folded a little over on each side, and then, marking a place with her hand on the sleeve, folded that back, and then back again. She brought the bottom half of the blouse up and, with a fast motion, turned the blouse right side up and placed it on the growing stack, each blouse the same crisp shape.

While they worked, Mother suggested that I make a sewing kit for Patt to take with her. I brought Mother's sewing basket from the dresser in her bedroom. Spools of different colors wound round and round its circle, and in the center a red tomato pin cushion, with its attached baby strawberry, sat spiky with needles and pins. I found an empty spool. Then I worked to find thread to match Patt's clothes. Carefully, I wrapped a little of the thread around the spool, making sure the different colors didn't run together. At the end, just for fun, I added a bright blue, my favorite color.

We helped Patt load the car. Father was helping Heinie bring in the last of his field corn, so John would get to drive Patt to Brookings. Bill would go along to keep John company on the return trip. Bob and I would have to stay home.

Then, when all the packing and hauling was done and we came out to give a last wave, there, between Patt and two boxes in the backseat, was Bob! I stuck out my tongue at him and he put his thumbs in his ears, grinned a silly grin, and waggled his fingers.

Mother and I stood by the house as the car went down the driveway. Just as it turned the curve near the old cottonwood tree, John gave three short beeps on the horn and I saw Patt's hand waving out the window.

As my older siblings left the farm, I became increasingly restless. At age eleven, I'd not yet had a chance to travel. So I was excited, and more than a little nervous, when Helen invited me to visit her in Minneapolis. There, she took me to the top of the twenty-nine-story Foshay Tower, where I viewed a city for the first time, and to the famous department stores, Dayton's and Donaldson's. More awe-inspiring was lunch at the Chinese Palace, where I was equally enthralled by the abundance of scarlet brocade and the intricately carved chairs and tables. Less so by the chow mein and egg drop soup.

UP THE WHETSTONE RIVER,
SLOWLY

The summer preceding our senior year of high school, my friend Josie and I were feeling stifled by the expectations and restrictions imposed upon us. We felt constrained by the mold we'd been placed into: good girls who excel at school.

"Let's do something exceptional," I told her. "Something no one will expect from us."

"What would that be?" she replied.

We discussed possibilities. A few days later, we'd come up with a plan. On an August morning, we packed a lunch and a thermos of water and slipped out of Josie's house to the shore of Big Stone Lake, where her family's canoe was moored at the dock.

Our plan was to paddle to the mouth of the lake, then up the Whetstone River, where, after a few hours of easy paddling, we'd pull up, triumphant, at the Big Rock on the river near our house.

The sky was cloudless, the lake clear. As we settled into the rhythm of paddling, startled ducks flapped into the air, leaving bluish-green streaks on the water.

I began to sing, "Row, row, row your boat gently down the stream . . ."

"You know we aren't rowing, right?" Josie said with a smile. Then she joined in and we sang as we paddled.

After an hour or so, the flow of water diminished. Our leisurely pace ended as we were forced to maneuver the canoe away from shallow water to avoid becoming grounded. The sun rose higher and beat down upon us. Then we came to a long tumble of rocks.

"What do we do now?" I asked.

"We'll have to carry it over the rocks," Josie replied matter-of-factly.

But the canoe was heavy, and we had to drag it.

The river narrowed. Trees on the banks drooped over the water, but their shade offered no relief. Without sunlight, the humidity increased. Mosquitoes began to attack our ankles and arms.

There were almost no signs of civilization, only a few strands of barbed wire attached to rotting fence posts that a flood had dislodged long ago.

"How much farther is your farm?" Josie asked.

"Oh, it can't be far," I said, but in truth I'd never been to this part of the river and I had no idea how much farther we had to go.

Even though Josie must have found this information unsettling, she didn't complain or blame me. We both had thought this was a great idea. We continued on. Now we were pulling the canoe more often than paddling it. Our feet became scratched from the rocks; our arms began to turn red.

Then, around a curve, we were dismayed to see a large oak toppled across the river. There was no way we could lift the canoe over the tree's trunk and its tangled branches.

"What do we do now?" we asked in unison.

"I think we have to give up," Josie said.

"Oh no! My brothers will laugh at us!"

"And how will I get the canoe back before my father comes home from work?" Josie said.

Dispiritedly, we dragged the canoe up onto the bank and placed it on a relatively flat spot.

"Okay, I'll lead the way," I said.

With Josie following me, I struggled through weeds and around bushes. Eyes ever alert for poison ivy, we trudged on.

As soon as we reached the spot on the river where the white bridge had once stood, we heard Coal's excited yipping. By the time we reached the cool shade of the cottonwood tree at the beginning of the drive, he was already there, with his wet nose and wagging tail, to greet us. We'd made it.

When we entered the kitchen after what seemed like hours, we probably looked like amateur explorers who'd been lost and just staggered out of a jungle. I know we looked really bad, because my brothers held their teasing in check.

"We need help," I told them. And then, as best I could, I described where we'd abandoned the canoe. Bill and Bob hitched a trailer to the Ford tractor. They drove to the neighbor's, and while Bill drove along the edge of the field, Bob walked on the slope of the bank so he could view the river's edge. When he spied the canoe, the two of them hauled it to the top and secured it with rope to the trailer.

When they returned to our yard, Bill yelled at me, "Get in the car! Follow us to town."

With Josie as passenger, I drove our car behind the tractor and its unusual load to Josie's.

On the way, Josie turned to me and said, "Canoeing up the river wasn't a good idea."

"Correction," I replied. "It was just plain dumb."

When school began a few days later, I wrote about the episode and titled it "Canoodling Up the River." My English teacher gave me an A plus.

That wasn't the first time I'd made a foolish decision. There had been the previous winter, when my friend Flo and I had responded to Dick Bonn's request. He was the star athlete at our high school, and my first crush. He had a job delivering milk to the families in town before school each morning, but he had to be away for a week because of a basketball tournament. He'd already asked his boss for time off a few times before.

"I think I'll lose my job if I ask again," he told Flo and me. "And I need the money. Will the two of you fill in for me?"

We couldn't resist the offer. Flo devised a reason to tell her parents why she had to stay with me that week, and I came up with one for mine. Dick told us where to pick up the milk and scribbled out a list of customers.

The night before our first run, Flo and I planned. Then we looked at each other in dismay. After we'd factored in the time it would take to drive from my place to town, pick up the milk, and deliver it, all before eight, we realized we'd have to get up at three-thirty in the morning!

When we set out on that first cold, dark morning, I felt that same eerie sensation I'd had as a little girl when all of us piled into the car to go to Mass while the stars were still bright in the sky.

I'd driven my father's two-ton truck plenty of times before, so I became the designated driver. This open-sided milk truck took a little getting used to because it was top-heavy. By the third day, we'd found our rhythm. I'd pull up to a house and keep the motor idling while Flo grabbed the wire carrier, hopped down, dashed to the doorstep, dropped off the milk, grabbed the empty bottles, ran back, and slid into the truck. Then I'd shift gears and let up on the clutch, and off we'd go to the next home.

On the fourth morning when we stepped out of my house, Flo and I saw that everything was coated in ice. I had to drive much more slowly. Flo couldn't dash but instead had to place each foot just so—these were glass bottles she was carrying.

As we approached the last house on our route, we were congratulating ourselves on having had no accidents, no broken bottles, until, that is, we remembered the dog. The house sat on a steep slope, with twenty or so steps leading up to the front door. This dog didn't just have a threatening bark—it bit! On the first days, Flo had enough time before the dog could reach her to dash through the snow. That was faster than going down the steps. But that day, as everything was covered in ice, running was out of the question. In the truck, we considered our problem and made a mutual decision. The Hansens didn't get their milk that morning.

THE SOCIAL WORKER

B eing the youngest (and a girl) was definitely a disadvantage. Once my sisters had left, I was the perfect target for
my brothers—verbally and physically. John is honest. He tells
with pride how he hit a bull's eye on a running target with his
slingshot. That target was me. I still remember the surprise of
his ambush and the sting of that stone on my shoulder.

I've always hated being labeled as the "baby of the family."
I still wear that mantle. Milestone ages for others have been
celebrated with fanfare—fifty, sixty, seventy. But when I
reached those birthdays, honoring those years had become a
ho-hum affair.

But long before that, when I returned to the farm on college breaks, my lowly spot proved to be a gift. There were times
then when I had Mother all to myself. I'd help her with the
chores, and then, because her workload had lessened, she'd feel
free to take a break.

"Let's go for a ride," I'd say.

"Oh, that sounds nice," she'd reply.

My mother never learned to drive. Doing so, with those
first automobiles, required a balletic set of movements—juggling

the choke, the gas, the gears, and, of course, the brakes, all at the same time. My mother wanted to drive, but when, during her first lesson with my father, she backed into a field and leveled a portion of the oats crop, she never tried again.

Happy with my invitation, my mother would change her dress and put on a dab of lipstick, and the two of us would climb into our '49 Ford. Off we'd go. My father would be in the yard, making repairs to some farm machine. Now my mother was the one going to town! With a smile, she'd wave goodbye to him as I accelerated toward the cottonwood tree and the turn up the hill.

We headed to Ortonville, parked, and walked by Mamee's, a small dress shop. The owner carried the latest fashions. We paused for a few moments to admire the styles in the windows. Then we continued on to Penney's, where we browsed the aisles. Depending on the season, I may have taken time to search for a formal dress to wear to a campus ball.

The prices were right. One time I found an amazing evening dress that I could afford. Only three dollars! A sapphire-blue satin sheath with spaghetti straps and a chiffon top of the same color to cover up, for that time, too much bare skin. I wish I'd kept that dress.

After that, we walked to the café on the next block and ordered coffee and cookies. Cookies someone else had baked—a pleasure for my mother.

I know that I did more than my share of talking, confiding in my mother, voicing my concern over this or that. I seem always to have been the worrying type. I tell myself that if I worry enough about something, it won't happen. In my experience, it's what I don't anticipate that turns out to be the most damaging.

A few times, when circumstances allowed us to be away from the farm for a substantial amount of time, we drove up the Minnesota side of Big Stone Lake on a narrow, twisty, tarred road that ridged the side of the cliff. The lack of a shoulder made the long drop to the rocky shore below all too apparent. I had to be alert for oncoming cars and trucks rounding the curves. But Mother was free to enjoy glimpses of the lake between tall evergreens and oaks. With the windows down, we breathed in the scent of the trees and heard the water lapping against the shore.

It was a point in her life when my mother finally had time to reflect, and I was there to listen, and so it was that I heard the story of the inspection.

Mother had been working in the kitchen when she heard a knock. When she opened the door, she was surprised to see a stranger—a stern-looking woman wearing a suit, hat, and gloves and carrying a satchel.

"I'd like to come in," the woman said, even before she'd introduced herself.

Mother was mortified. The kitchen was steamy and smelly from the weekly chore of doing the laundry. She didn't want anyone to see her home looking this way, certainly not a stranger. But she had no choice.

"Please come in," she said.

"I understand you have a child here who is not normal."

My mother was shocked; she could only nod her head.

"Well, I'm from the county. I'm here to check your home," she said.

And before my mother had time to react, the woman strode through the kitchen and into the dining room.

A triumphant "Aha!" was followed by "Well, here's the poor creature!"

My mother was unable to speak. The woman pulled a sheaf of papers from her satchel and began to ask questions. "How often do you feed her? What do you feed her?"

After three or four of these kinds of questions, Mother outlined the care she gave Dorothy every day.

"Well," the woman said, "we may have to remove her."

With that, my mother took over. She spoke in short, clipped sentences. Not her way at all.

"That's it! I give Dorothy the best care. You will never take her. No one will ever take her from me! Dorothy is staying right here!"

And then, for the first and only time, my mother escorted a visitor to the door without offering a cup of coffee.

It was not that day but during that same period of time that she told me something that happened years later. This, too, must have been haunting her all those years.

"The sisters asked us to come up," she said. "Dorothy was crying out, obviously in great pain. Her screams were disturbing patients on another floor. The nuns said they could no longer keep her. We told them we couldn't take her back. Roy couldn't work if he wasn't able to sleep. And, she continued, "All of you needed your rest, or you wouldn't be able to do your schoolwork. We were so grateful when they found a place for her. Even if it *was* in the basement."

My parents became accustomed to saying goodbye, though perhaps the finality of that gesture reminded my mother of the pain of saying goodbye to Dorothy.

In turn, John, Bill, and Bob set out. My mother baked and packed cookies to send to South Korea, where John was stationed as a helicopter pilot. The armistice had been declared, but bombs were still exploding where his battalion was located. She did the same for Bill, though she probably didn't worry quite as much. He was stationed in Germany, on a familiar continent, and with adequate supplies of all necessities.

Bob stayed closer to home—Minnesota, North Dakota, Indiana—and thus was able to visit my parents more often. He'd call before his arrival, alerting my mother that he'd be there in time for the evening meal.

And then I, the youngest, left.

THE NIGHT
THE BARN BURNED

It took less than a minute from the scratch of the match, its first leap of flame, to follow the rough splatter of gasoline through bits and pieces of dried alfalfa across the floor to the remaining store of last summer's hay, there to explode, making a huge ball of fire and with it enough light to announce its awful presence.

In the nearest farmhouse, the widow Mattie Snyder was talking on the party line, discussing the right time to begin planting her garden.

In Big Stone, Jack Cloos, a volunteer fireman, was hunched over the oak bar in Redice's Tavern, feeling a little guilty as he sipped a Hamm's beer. He'd left his wife, Joan with their young children, ironing clothes, including a white shirt for him to wear to Mass the next morning.

Also in town, Ed Mounce was sitting at a small desk in his dining room, adding up receipts his wife had left in the cracked glass chicken-shaped dish on the kitchen counter. He planned to get a head start. Three days remained before the first of the month. If his wife had spent more than her month's household allowance, he'd know how much to deduct from next month's.

Back on our farm, a man, half-crazed with anger and alcohol, lurched back and stopped to admire his work. Jim Wellburn was a man who drank too much and, as a result, couldn't keep a job. Needing an extra hand after his sons left home, and with a desire to help the man's family, my father hired him on a part-time basis. But as Jim had proved less and less reliable, my father had become more and more frustrated and had recently fired him.

As he ran across the hog yard and into the trees, Jim may have felt a strange exuberance knowing, at last, that he'd done something irreversible, splendid, something the people on this farm and in the town would never forget. He struggled through brush, stomping on emergent poison ivy, and slipped and slid down the riverbank only a few hundred yards from his former boss.

My father, Roy, sat in the kitchen of the simple farmhouse at the counter he and his neighbor Heinie had made. They'd rebuilt the entire kitchen together, designing the small space so that Myrtle, my mother, would scarcely have to move, would need only to turn around to dip out the flour from a drop-down bin, or take just a short step to retrieve the milk from the refrigerator as she made her bread and her famous sweet rolls. They'd worked together when Heinie was still at his peak, still smoking two packs of Lucky Strikes a day, before emphysema started withholding oxygen, robbing Heinie of his spirit and Roy of Heinie's companionship.

Roy's hair was wet and covered by a net Myrtle had devised shortly after they'd gotten married, almost forty years before. The first week after they'd returned from their short wedding trip, she had seen how, after a shampoo, his hair, black and thick with glints of silver, ballooned out over his ears and above his forehead, making him look foolish. She went into their bedroom, returned with one leg of hose, and, after assuring him that she couldn't wear it because of a wide run, snipped it in two. Then, tying one end in a tight knot, she gently worked the other over his poufed-out hair. That night—the night the barn would burn—Roy sat with wet hair, contained by Myrtle's ingenuity and gentle hands, drinking his ninth, and, he thought, last, cup of coffee of the day.

Marian, Myrtle's sister—almost a twin, only ten months separated them—who had driven six hours from Pierre that day so she could say goodbye to Barbara, her youngest niece, stood by the gas range, carefully layering pieces of homemade bread with hot wild plum sauce. She never could understand her nieces' and nephews' passion for wild plum cobbler, but the next night was to be Barbara's farewell dinner, and, even though the cobbler was best served in winter, having been chilled to teeth-tingling coldness on the porch, it had been Barbara's dessert request.

Marian thought back to the time when Myrtle telephoned her to tell her she was pregnant once again, with Barbara, as it so happened. Marian had congratulated her sister, but after she'd hung up she'd rested her head on the phone box and wept. Roy and Myrtle already had six children and one of those, Dorothy, the oldest, had been damaged at birth, so she never could walk or talk. She died a painful death at age nineteen.

How old had Barbara been when Dorothy died? Six? Seven? On that long-ago night, after Marian had hung up the phone, she could think of nothing good about the birth of one more child. She'd questioned God's wisdom, but Barbara's birth had turned out to be a wonderful thing. Now, years later, here was Barbara, having earned a college degree, ready to set off around the world, not worried at all about what her decision to join the Peace Corps would bring.

President Kennedy had asked young people to help by going to countries around the world, and Barbara couldn't wait to be on her way. She'd already gone through training and studied the language. When Marian had driven into the farmyard earlier that day, Barbara had run to the car and said hello in Thai as she dipped down and raised her hands to her face in the traditional Thai greeting. Then she'd laughed and given Marian her usual hug.

Earlier that evening, when Marian had been alone with Myrtle, she'd asked her how she felt about Barbara's going off so far, for such a long time.

"I'm just happy for her. It's a wonderful opportunity," Myrtle responded.

Marian didn't ask any more questions.

Barbara's clothes were upstairs, folded, ready to be packed, ready to follow her around the world to a country whose statistics they knew—latitude, longitude, capital—though they knew nothing about the life Barbara would live there.

On that May evening in 1963, I was in the kitchen. I'd just given my mother a shampoo and, in preparation for doing her hair, had piled a stack of metal rollers on the end of the counter, near the door. I'd brought a chair from the dining room and the footstool from the living room. With my mother comfortably ensconced, I tucked a faded pink towel under the neck of her dress and began drying her hair with another. As I started to comb her hair, I felt my mother relax and noticed the slight smile on her lips. She looked much younger than her sixty years.

"Oh, that felt good. Thank you, Barbara."

"It'll be a long time before I can do this again," I said softly. "You will remember to send me Marker's orange slices, won't you?"

"Oh, of course I will. You'll write often, won't you?"

"Oh, yes. Remember, I don't like the pale orange ones. They're like mush. Get the dark orange ones. They're more satisfying to chew."

Aunt Marian laughed. "Barbara you're the only connoisseur of candy orange slices I've ever met."

I laughed, too, and, waving the comb in swoops above my mother's head, asked in a fake French accent, "Now, how would Madame like to have zee hair set?"

"Nothing special. Nothing extravagant! Remember, we're going to ten o'clock Mass in the morning."

"Oh, let's have some fun. How about a Jackie Kennedy style?"

"Quiet!" my father's voice cut through our chatter. "What was that noise? Someone must be here."

"I'll get it, Dad." I put down the comb and walked to the door. I saw a bright light reflecting off our Ford parked near the house, appearing as though another car was driving in. Then, looking to the right, toward the driveway, I saw streaks of orange and red on the gravel. What was happening? Unwillingly, my eyes were pulled up.

"Oh my God! The barn's on fire!"

Towering flames, fed by the night air, were erupting through the roof. It was as if a giant's invisible hand were tugging them toward the night sky. I dashed to the phone. When I lifted the receiver, I heard someone talking.

"Hang up! Our barn's on fire!"

I punched the receiver's rest viciously and dialed 0, trying to reach Big Stone's operator. I tried again. The call didn't go through.

"I'm driving to town for help!"

I rushed to the door and, not feeling the gravel on my bare feet, ran to the car and started it up. As I skidded out, I saw my father running toward the barn. I floored the accelerator, and the car wobbled on two wheels as I took the curve by the old cottonwood tree. I drove faster than I'd ever driven the twisting dirt road. As I came to the approach to the highway at the edge of town, I heard a wailful sound. It turned my stomach and brought a sour taste to my mouth.

"Farm fire," the siren announced to neighboring farms, to the town, to the volunteer firemen, to Jack Cloos, well into his third Hamm's, to Ed Mounce, who had almost figured out to the exact penny how much his wife had exceeded her allowance.

Hoping I was making the right decision, hoping there wasn't another farm fire this night, this hour, I yanked the steering wheel around. I knew if I didn't return down the narrow road before the fire engines I would be trapped out, trapped from my parents and the horrible thing that was happening to our farm.

I took the same curves and twists of the road as fast as I had a few minutes before. I didn't think of what I was driving toward, only concentrated so that the car would stay on the road. Beginning the drive up the back side of the pigpen hill, I saw an eerie light. Behind me, the wails of the sirens made a strange dirge as they echoed around the curves, up and down the small hills. I let up on the accelerator only a little, just enough to make the curve by the old tree safely. Even though I didn't look toward the barn as I drove the last yards toward the house, the fact of the fire was there. Its light filled the space around me, reflecting off every shiny surface.

Before the motor had stopped its rumble, I was out of the car. I turned toward the light and heat. Flames had almost devoured the roof. With that, I saw our entire yard illuminated orange. I could see each tree, each leaf, it seemed, outlined with a deadly glow. The burning hay in the loft had set the beams on fire. Their strong, arched ribs were brilliant streaks of red against the black sky. They formed the shape of a monstrous cathedral.

And there was my father, diminished almost to doll size, silhouetted against the fire. I saw him lead two cows out of the blaze and slap their flanks. This familiar motion, one I had observed since I'd been able to toddle to the barn, was strangely comforting. Then my father turned and walked back into the burning building.

"Dad! Don't go back! Don't go back!"

He couldn't hear me, and I realized from the set of his shoulders, the force of his stride, that I could not stop him. He would never let his cows burn alive. I watched as the fire devoured beams, shingles, and studs. Twisted and bent the iron of the cows' stanchions. Twisted and blackened the stainless-steel separator that my mother had carefully polished that morning. Twisted and destroyed the basketball hoop nailed to a wall of the haymow.

Big Stone's two fire engines sirened to a stop. Men hopped off, canvas hoses unfurling behind them. I ran to the driver of the first engine. I recognized Jack Cloos from church.

"Dad's in there! He's gone back to get the cows."

"Man inside! Man inside!" he bellowed, and, following the first man, ran toward the burning building.

I stood frozen. Three cars, one right after the other, slammed to a halt next to me. I watched as firemen on each side of the barn's doorway pointed their hoses inward and then up, forming an arc of water that crossed in the air. Through that silvery arc emerged three cows, bellowing, heads rolling, eyes bulging, followed by my father. He was shouting and pounding the last cow with his fists, but I couldn't hear him above the roar of the fire.

There seemed to be a halo around his head. What was that? Then I remembered my mother had given my father a shampoo and knew that my mother's crafted hairnet was about to begin burning. Jack turned his hose on my father. I saw him stagger back, another fireman catch him before he fell. He held my father under his arms at an angle to the ground. My father's feet spun as he tried to stand. Gently, as if in slow motion, the firemen righted him. Jack led him toward me.

"Take care of your dad," Jack told me, before he ran back to the blaze.

My father leaned into me, panting. He was heavier than I expected, and I staggered back until we both rested on the rear bumper of the car.

"Dad! That was stupid." The sentence began as a rebuke but ended softly.

"Just as stupid as you. What were you doing, driving back and forth?"

"My call didn't go through. I drove to town for help."

"And met the trucks on the way?" Though his voice sounded tired, his tone was sarcastic.

I started to answer him but saw that he was dripping water and bits of ash, and he smelled.

"Your hair's been burned a bit."

"Yeah, I stink. Like singed chicken feathers. Smells like your mother's just plucked a bird and is getting it ready for dinner."

His mention of my mother seemed to energize him. "Go! Go check on her!"

I ran into the house, through the kitchen, into the dining room. The familiar space gleamed. In the strange light, each piece of furniture stood out, distinct. The buffet with its vase of lilac blossoms, now drooping from the heat. The dining table covered with the white linen cloth, freshly laundered and ironed, ready for my party. I ran upstairs.

"Mom! Marian!" There was no answer.

It was hot. Sweat ran down my forehead, between my breasts. I heard a sound I couldn't place. Was it raining? Could God possibly have intervened to save the barn? But the water wasn't coming as drops; it was coming in gushes, splashing on the floor through the open window. In one terrible moment, I realized the firemen had given up on the barn and were now aiming their hoses at the house, which was now in danger from airborne bits of burning debris, trying to save it. Then there was silence. The noise of the torrent of water stopped, and I heard shouting.

Jack was calling out orders: "We've run out of water. Take that truck and back it down the riverbank. Put the hoses in the river."

I looked out the window and saw Albert West, a city employee who was responsible for tending and polishing the fire engines.

"No! You're not going to use the new engine!"

The two men were moving toward each other as they shouted. Their voices rose in volume as they drew closer to each other.

"Why not? For God's sake!"

"Not the new engine! That barbed wire will ruin it."

"What?" Jack shouted back. "Why in hell do you think we bought it? To put it in a museum?"

Jack shoved Albert aside, climbed into the cab of the shiny truck, wheeled it around, and started backing it up. I heard a long, high screech as metal scraped against metal.

"Mom! Marian! Where are you?" I turned back toward the stairs. The thought that the steps might no longer exist paralyzed me. These stairs were an entryway to solitude, a passage to a place where no one followed. I ran down them in a daze.

Not able to face going out the kitchen door toward the flames, I turned to the south porch and went out onto the lawn. At the far end, under the trees, I saw, in the glow that filled every space of the curve of earth that held our farm, two small figures. I ran toward them.

"Mom, Marian, what are you doing!"

Marian said, "We brought your things for your trip down from your room. Your mother wanted to make sure they weren't ruined."

On the grass they'd laid the old spread from my bed. On it in neat piles were my blouses and skirts, still carefully folded, shoes lined up side by side, camera, film in its small black cylinders, dark glasses, Thai dictionary, and journal-to-be. Everything for my trip was there. In the house were my mother's silver and her delicately etched goblets, my parents' wedding photograph, graduation portraits of my brothers, sisters, and me, the only photo of Dorothy that existed, the only one that would ever be. Every material thing my mother valued.

It was close to sunrise when I climbed the stairs to bed. The window in my room faced the empty air where the barn had stood. My father had driven to town for a case of beer and given it to the firemen, who were staying to make sure the fire did not revive. I fell asleep to the men's laughter and sizzling sounds as they relieved themselves on the hot ashes.

The next morning, Jack Cloos, filthy and exhausted, slipped up the side aisle of St. Charles Borromeo Church ten minutes after Mass had begun to sit by the side of his wife, their children clean and crisp on her right. That afternoon, the miser Ed Mounce had to forgo fishing so that he could figure his wife's account one more time. My party took place as planned, minus the wild plum cobbler and mother's famous sweet rolls, all of which the firemen had devoured the night before. Marian returned to her job in Pierre one day late. She called her employer and told him what had happened, and thus was able to stay and wave goodbye to me at the Aberdeen airport.

A tall barn was never rebuilt; the cost of lumber made it prohibitive. A one-story concrete barn was constructed in its place.

My mother and father worked on.

On one of the planes I boarded on my long trip to Thailand— the last, from Hong Kong to Bangkok—I leaned back and the happenings of the night the barn burned returned. I saw the towering flames, the awful beauty of the fire, and my pulse raced. Saw my shoes lined up carefully on the grass and again felt grateful for what my mother and aunt had done, but that gratitude was tinged with a nagging sense of inadequacy. Did I measure up to these two women whom I loved so much? Tears rolled down my cheeks, and I turned to the window so my seatmate wouldn't notice.

As I searched for a tissue, I struggled to find the tab on the zipper of my bag. When I felt the metal, I thought of my father that night. How had he managed to open the stanchions to free the cows? The iron must have been red hot. I heard again the tone of his voice as he asked me why I'd driven to town. Would I ever please him?

The events of the night continued to spin in my mind. I wanted, desperately needed, to do something physical, to get up and move around. I longed to go for a walk. A walk along the river.

AN UNFORESEEN PLEASURE

＞

When he reached the age of seventy, my father began to liquidate his farm animals. He resisted getting rid of the cows for a long time, but being tied to the essential twice-a-day milkings had become too restrictive. When there had been at least one child at home, he'd had freedom to take short trips. More than once when my parents traveled, that necessary chore had fallen to me; I'd always managed to enlist a friend to help with that onerous task.

At last, he sold his beloved Holsteins. With that action, no domestic animals remained. There wasn't even our faithful black Lab, Coal, to keep my parents company. After she'd been hit by a car, Coal always walked with a sideways limp; as she aged, her black coat became sprinkled with gray, but she continued to announce visitors with throaty, nonthreatening barks. Coal always ran to greet me, her tail wagging so hard it could throw me off balance. When, returning for a short visit, I climbed out of the car and there was no Coal, I sensed the worst immediately.

Before I'd even hugged my mother hello, I asked, "Where's Coal?"

"Oh, Barbara. She's gone. She came to the door one day and indicated she was thirsty. I refilled her water dish, and when

I stepped out a little later, the pan was half empty but there was no sign of Coal. I called her. No response. She'd wandered off into the woods. She knew she was dying and didn't want to be any bother to us."

Then there were no animals. My father only occasionally rode the tractor. It was very quiet.

Deer started coming closer and closer to the house. In all seasons, my mother often stopped working to observe their interactions. Wood ducks nested in natural cavities of the oak trees at the edge of our lawn. The male duck's plumage is often said to be the most resplendent of all the waterfowls'.

After she had poured my father a cup of coffee, my mother got into the habit of pouring a cup for herself, too. In the house, looking out, they could talk without frightening the birds. Together they'd point to and then watch the male wood duck as he flew back and forth, feeding the ducklings. My mother would have been well aware that, though invisible among the foliage and thickets, the dun-colored female bird was working just as hard as the male to feed their hungry offspring. They'd admire the bird's head, a kabuki-like mask of jet black enhanced by delicate lines of white set below a helmet of emerald green. All of that was highlighted by an orange bill, red eyes, and a surprising swatch of purple.

The two of them agreed. Mother Nature had put her best effort into crafting this regal bird.

With the unfamiliar quiet had come an unexpected reward.

DIRT

‿⟶

Before they left their native countries, some immigrants packed a handful of dirt in a small box to carry with them to their new homes.

All of us seem to have packed a bit of the earth from our father's farm, which had been *his* father's farm, into our souls before we scattered away from that small, none-too-prosperous homestead, across the United States, around the world, into our financially and emotionally varied states of success.

Or maybe we didn't have to pack it. That soil had worked its way into the center of each of us.

Helen's dirt is identical to my mother's dark earth, moist at the surface from a light spring rain or from careful watering during a hot, dry summer. Earth from the edge of Mother's tomato plants, bearing their fragile white blossoms and the pungent aroma of their leaves. Earth from under the large peony plants that grew where the lawn met the flower garden. Plants that bore blossoms whose sweet scent was strong enough to mask the odor that wafted down from the barn, where the men struggled to clean out a winter's accumulation.

Earth: rich, moist, verdant. Mother had faith that with care, no matter the hailstorms or droughts, or early frosts, her plants would thrive and flower. She believed that was true of people as well. Helen does also.

Patt's handful would be the dirt that she swept, dusted, and washed out of our house. The dirt she battled. The same dirt, it seemed to her, over and over, week after week. The wind blew it in where the windows didn't fit tight. The men brought it in from the fields and the barns, stomping some of it off in the little entryway before they entered the kitchen but shedding more, from their jackets and pants, shirts and bodies, once they were in the house.

One time, when John and Bill were not yet in their teens, they carefully filled the pockets of their work pants and then deliberately emptied them out on the kitchen's shiny linoleum floor, which had just been washed and waxed. They ran, if not for their lives, at least to escape grave bodily damage. And Patt, who never cried, wept in frustration. She never forgave them. She still talked about it fifty years later.

Banishing dirt was Patt's obsession, her religion. She expended not only time but all of her strength on her quest. If you'd met her, you might have noticed that her biceps were out of proportion with her slim frame.

John, I think, probably packed a chunk of dirt twined through with roots from the bank of the river. He laid his trap lines there each winter, fished from its banks each summer, and, generous with his time as a high school senior, took his kid brother and sister ice skating, guiding Bob and me down the twisting, treacherous river by a full moon's light. That night was as close to perfection as a few hours can be. I realize I've never mentioned that to him.

Bill's dirt would be from the most fertile land of our small farm, the South Forty—land he coaxed to yield, during various years, flax, soybeans, corn, alfalfa. My grandfather had loaned John and Bill enough money to buy a Ford tractor, and with that trusty tractor and that piece of land, Bill was determined to work his way to a place where he never had to borrow money again. Some summer nights as a young teenager, I fell asleep to the sound of the tractor, piloted by Bill, its lights on full beam, roaring away and returning, roaring away and returning. Always returning.

Perhaps Bob's came from the pigpen hill. Earth baked hard, bleached brown, with little pieces of rock running through it. Earth that never yielded more than patches of grass and an amazing variety of weeds. When we were very young, Bob, perhaps only four, and I, only two, climbed that hill, where we picked blossoms of one of those weeds, yellow mustard, which we presented excitedly to our mother. Through adversity, he's come up with joy. In our storytelling, teasing clan, he is without rival.

As he told a shaggy-dog story, Bob kept a motel room full of us quiet for half an hour as he built to the punch line. In that disheartening room, my sisters, my brothers, three sisters-in-law, and I erupted into laughter. We laughed until the people next door pounded on the wall and Patt complained he'd made her wet her pants.

This, on the night before our father's funeral.

Mine? Earth, dust, soil, loam, clay, mud. Who else but the writer in our family would ever spend so much time thinking about all these different words for dirt?

And which dirt would I take from that farm I long to return to?

In my small box, I'd pack some from the ravine, which stayed green even during a long, dry summer. The ravine where I hurried each day in May after school. The only place where all the violets bloomed—lavender, purple, white, yellow—and where, a few weeks later, buds of columbines opened into small chandeliers of red and gold. Earth that demanded I use my patience and memory, so that when I returned the next spring or summer to the right spot at the right time and found the violets of different hues, each on its own timetable, I was not surprised, but rather rewarded and renewed.

But how could I have gotten to me—the youngest, the last, the end of the line, the baby—without writing about the person for whom the dirt of that small farm was most vital? My father. My father, who struggled all his adult life to work that dirt, trying to provide enough food and dollars for our family of nine.

He worked just to keep the dirt in place. In the '30s, he watched in despair as his rich topsoil blew eastward, far beyond his farm and neighboring Minnesota. After ten years, the Great Drought finally came to an end. Some years, the spring rains merged with melting snow, transforming our quiet stream into rampaging torrents that often overran its banks. After the water receded, my father would walk the fields, head down, shoulders drooping, to survey the damage. He'd kick at the layers of jetsam: gravel, twigs and branches, rocks, and, among it all, unseen seeds, which the following summer would yield a frustrating assortment of weeds.

For him I'd pack a handful of the dirt he'd picked up after a crop-saving July rain. Dirt from a freshly tilled stand of field corn. I can see him squat, reach down with his large hands, reddened from years of work in the sun, pick up a handful, raise it to his face, and inhale the sweet smell of his land, his life.

Now, have I included everyone? No, there's Dorothy.

She never felt dirt beneath her bare feet, never fell, skinning her knees on bits of gravel, never had the fun of making mud pies, the matter oozing through her fingers. I'll give her those and add the dust mites that, when the light was just right, glittered and sparkled as they danced above her crib.

VI. RETURNING
AGAIN AND AGAIN

THE MOURNING DOVE

As a small child
I rode with my father at twilight
down clover-fringed dirt roads
to check the fields of grain.
I asked him
what made that lovely, lonely sound
again and again.
The mourning dove, he told me.
How can a morning dove sing
at this time of day?
And then my father
Tried to tell me of mourning.

ANOTHER GOODBYE

⌒

1983

As the kneelers were raised, their collective rumble echoed through the church.

"Let us pray," the priest intoned, and everyone stood for the final blessing.

It was the end of another funeral in the white clapboard church that stood on the western edge of my small hometown. Its spire reached into the late-morning sky, toward what I hoped was the direction of heaven.

What was the first funeral I attended in this church? That would have been my sister Dorothy's. I was seven. It was horrible. I sat alone and confused. All my brothers and sisters were in the front row, side by side, with my mother and father. I was in the row behind them, wedged between my aunt and uncle, whom I didn't even know. I sat, knelt, stood. Up and down I went. I tried hard not to cry, but the tears streamed down my cheeks anyway. I made a noise as I tried to keep my nose from running. My aunt turned toward me and frowned.

"Blow your nose," she whispered, as she handed me a small white handkerchief.

My husband, Joe, gave me a nudge, and I returned to this day, this service. It was time for our sons to join their cousins for the recessional. All the male grandchildren were honorary pallbearers for this service, my mother's funeral.

I had been the last of my family to arrive for the viewing, three days earlier, after a long, exhausting trip from New York. Appropriate, I supposed. I'd been the last born, the last to leave home. I'd hoped to have some time alone with my mother, but that would be impossible. I was lucky we'd arrived before the end of visiting hours.

When Joe, our two sons, Peter and Stephen, and I had pulled up to the large white house, it had already been dark for two hours. Tall columns flanked the doorway. I opened the back door of the car and helped my sons out, then crouched down so I could look into their faces.

"You don't have to go see Grand-mère if you don't want to. There's another room where you can sit and wait. As soon as Daddy is able to leave, he'll take you back to the motel. If the pool's still open, you can go swimming."

As I told them that, a little crack in my wall of grief allowed me to be amazed that the run-down motel in this small town in South Dakota had an indoor swimming pool.

Neither Peter nor Stephen said anything. Realizing how scared and sad they were that I was leaving them in this strange place in such painful circumstances, even if only for a short time, brought tears to my eyes. Then I noticed that Stephen was tightly clutching his brother's hand. *They have each other*, I thought, as I turned and led the way.

The scent of greenhouse flowers and a faint smell of chemicals pushed out as I opened the door. I saw my sister Patt right away. Helen was a little farther back. I didn't have to call to them; they'd been waiting. And, as though it were their only purpose that evening, they came to me. As Patt stepped to my left and Helen to my right, my daily role of mother slipped away. I was kid sister again, and Helen, Patt, and I were one. We would never speak to our mother again. I no longer had to hide my grief. I sobbed into their warm bodies.

We have each other, I told myself.

"We'll take you to her," they said.

Seeing the three of us together, relatives and neighbors silently stepped back into the vestibule. And one more time we four women shared the same room.

Three days later, at the funeral, my pain had not dulled. I stood up automatically, trying not to weep openly as all of us waited for the priest to speak. My mother's casket rested a short way from me. Forever closed.

There was a slight delay. The organ didn't burst into its usual rich tones. My brother Bob got up and walked to the front of the church. His words were clear, but the familiar rhythm of his sentences was missing. He sounded plodding. There would be no punch line. He was making a request on behalf of the parish.

"Because of the extremely muddy conditions, please don't drive into the cemetery. Park on the county road and walk to the grave site."

Bedridden and confused, my father wasn't able to be present, but my brother's request added a practical note that he would have appreciated. In fact, he'd probably prefer that no one even disturb the sodden grass.

"What's all this fuss about?" he would say, "Mother's gone. What difference does any of this make?"

The funeral director touched my shoulder.

"It's time now. Put their parkas on."

I did so, and then the director led my two young sons up the side aisle toward my mother's coffin. An icy blast of air reached me as the church doors were opened wide. Peter reached for Stephen's hand, and then the two of them, leading their older cousins, followed my mother as she left the church for the last time.

My chest hurt. I resolved to visit my father as soon as all of this was over.

THE FINAL FLOOD

The summer following my mother's death, my siblings and I juggled the timing of our visits to our father so that he'd have company more frequently.

So when Joe and I traveled to South Dakota with our boys, the first thing on my agenda was to visit my father. I set the alarm in our motel room for five and then awakened early to turn it off so it wouldn't disturb anyone. I had laid out my clothes before going to bed so I could dress quietly, and I heard only soft, rhythmic breathing and a few muffled snores from my sons and husband as I closed the door and locked it behind me.

My father had always started his day at 6:00 a.m. That was in the dark winter months. In July he would have been up at five, latest. I was hoping that I'd see him at his best at this early hour.

The melancholy song of a mourning dove floated across a field on the other side of the highway. Many of the landmarks had changed. Even the highway followed a new, strange route. But this morning the air, the light, and a familiar bird welcomed me.

The eastern sky stilled me for a moment. Wide ribbons of vivid purple and orange lay along the horizon, and overhead wispy drifts of clouds reflected faint variations of those colors on a great comforter of soft blue.

The night before, for a few miles out of Big Stone City, the route of the highway had been familiar. Glancing to the left, I'd seen a light glimmering through the trees, but it had not been a welcoming sight, as it once had been. It gave out a lonely feeling. The light came from the building that had been my parents' home all those years, now remodeled and modernized, now a dwelling for strangers.

Five minutes later, the road was foreign to me—wide, straight, and level. Gone were the gently rolling hills, the winding curves, the dips that my brothers, driving our old Ford, liked to take a little too fast, so that my stomach lagged behind the rest of my body, landing with a thud when the road leveled out.

Also gone was the infamous "twelve-mile corner." I wondered if the cluster of seven white wooden crosses that had been erected to memorialize veterans who were killed in World War II still stood there. Once, they had caused all but the most callous of speeders to lift a foot from the accelerator for a brief moment.

I decided to walk the short way to the nursing home, but as I left the motel parking lot I realized that the outskirts of this small town had been designed for drivers, not pedestrians. I was forced to walk along the edge of the highway. A large semi trailer whooshed by me, throwing up dirt and gravel, and I stepped farther off the road. I was now walking through tall grasses, their tops bowed down with bushy heads. Soon my hair, where it rested on the back of my neck, was wet. It would be a typical South Dakota summer day: sunny, windy, and hot.

The smell of newly mown hay from a nearby field caught me by surprise, and I remembered a summer day when I had stepped out our kitchen door and saw my brothers bringing the baled hay into the barn. Alone, I'd been on my way to pick strawberries, a quiet, wearying, never-ending job, and I'd resented my brothers' camaraderie, the noise and heft of their work, the tangible nature of their accomplishments.

I walked up the concrete path to the nursing home. Everything was clipped and neat. A revolving sprinkler sent iridescent sparkles of life-giving water onto the lawn. Another dry summer. How we worried about water all those years.

I opened the door to the facility and stepped in. The air was cool but felt dead. At the end of a long corridor, a small nun dressed in a traditional habit sat at a desk, writing in a logbook.

"Excuse me. Good morning."

"Good morning." Her eyes seemed to scan my flesh and soul in a glance.

"I'm Roy Hoffbeck's daughter Barbara. Is it all right if I visit him now?"

"Well, you're here bright and early. But that's okay—you can see him before his bath."

I had forgotten how informal, easy, things were out here.

"I have to warn you, though, his mind's not always right. He just doesn't want to accept the fact that your mother's gone. Keeps asking us why we won't let him see her. If he talks that way today, don't encourage him. He has to learn to accept reality."

"Which room is he in?"

"Down the hall to the right. His name's on the door."

As I walked down the hall, I saw a rectangular cork bulletin board on the wall opposite me. A smiling sun made of yellow construction paper was thumbtacked to the upper left corner. Affixed below that was "Today is Saturday, July 9," each word on a separate piece of paper to allow for appropriate changes. "The weather forecast is sunny." It still announced yesterday's date.

Along the bottom were several childlike flowers cut out of red and blue construction paper. I remembered how one especially dry summer years before, not wanting to use precious cistern water for flowers, my mother had carried pots of cooled cooking water out to her parched zinnias and marigolds. And there had been another year, after hearing an early frost warning, when my mother, after covering the tomato vines and their not-yet-ripened greenish-orange fruit with an old blanket, placed another atop her valiant end-of-summer flowers. These paper flowers—parodies of nature—were what my mother had looked at in her last months! I had an urge to tear them off the board and toss them into the wastebasket.

As I turned at the end of the hall, I saw my father's name printed in black marker on heavy white paper slipped into a brass holder on an open door. It was a doleful reminder of his transient status here.

I stepped into the room quietly, not wanting to disturb him if he were still asleep.

I stopped abruptly, my mind unable to accept the figure I saw in the bed as my father. The forceful, independent man I remembered was struggling, now a prisoner.

His wrists were tied to the bed with white cloth strips. That was the first thing I saw. That, and the shades pulled down to keep out the early-morning light. I leaned close to his face and spoke more loudly than normal. His hearing had improved after a stroke some years back, but words seemed to blur together for him.

"Good morning, Dad."

"Barbara." He breathed out my name, a statement, not a question, so I knew that he recognized me.

I took his hand—all bones, it seemed, covered by pale pink rice paper—and bent to kiss his hollow cheek. He clasped my hand hard. I was surprised at his strong grip.

"You'd still be able to milk a cow by hand if you had to."

He laughed a slow laugh. "I could do a lot of things if they'd let me out of this damn place."

I noticed that his eyes were still the color of the sky at noon in January, and, though his hair was silvery white, it was still thick.

"I don't think that'll be possible for a time, but at least we can get rid of these while I'm here." I concentrated on untying the cloth strips. Then I moved toward the window.

I remembered how my father had always been looking at the sky, sensing the air—looking for the first gathering of clouds in a dry summer; a ring around a winter's moon that would foretell snow; a certain combination of heat, humidity, and stillness that warned of a twister. The air and the sky had been his life's companions. And his enemies.

"There's the most beautiful sky this morning," I said, and reached over to raise the shade.

The conditioned air hummed through my father's room, and, looking up, I saw that his small portion of the morning sky contained no hint of the glorious colors above the horizon.

I turned back to the room. It was the size of an overgrown closet. On a small dresser, a miniature live Christmas tree still stood—green at the top, but with yellow boughs at the bottom. Attached were several miniature candy canes and a small Santa waving a bell in his hand.

My eyes turned to a plastic frame holding photos of different sizes and shapes: babies, brides and grooms, graduates, all of them smiling. A picture of my two boys in a brotherly hug filled one corner.

"How've you been, Dad?"

"A hell of a lot better than they want me to be."

"Well, you did give us a scare."

"I'm tough. I'll go when I'm ready to go."

"You always were a stubborn man," I replied in a teasing manner.

"Not as stubborn as you. Traipsing after a dream, then not coming back."

I opened my mouth to speak and immediately closed it.

"Way off there. You hardly saw your mother in her last years."

Tears came to my eyes. He'd hit a nerve. I still felt guilty and bereft because I hadn't been able to visit my mother more often during her final years, and it had become impossible for us to communicate over the phone.

My mother had had Parkinson's disease, and she could no longer walk or dress herself, but worse for me was that the disease had weakened her vocal muscles so she couldn't speak loudly enough to be understood. When I telephoned her from New York, she'd answer my questions. I'd ask, "What?" a time or two, and sense her frustration as she tried to speak more loudly, more clearly, but I heard only scratchy sounds coming from the earpiece. No matter how I tried, I just couldn't understand what she was saying. I'd pretend I did and then fill in the silence with stories about Peter and Stephen. It would take me days to recover emotionally from those calls.

For what would be our last time together, she was in pain and hallucinating. She told me she wanted to see my father. In a cruel sleight of fate's hand, he was in critical condition in the same hospital. When I explained that to her, her panic overcame the disease's effects and, thinking of Dorothy, she cried out, "Do they have him in the basement?"

Now on this day with my father, I heard a rustle down the hall and saw a nurse with a basin.

"Looks like it's time for your bath," she told my father.

I turned toward the doorway.

"Now, don't run off just because I tell the truth. Is that all that you know how to do? Run away from hard things?"

"Joe will bring the boys over to see you about eleven." My voice sounded hollow, but my father either didn't notice or thought the fact not worth mentioning. "I'll stop by again this afternoon."

I walked down the hall to a small room near the front door, trying to decide if I should leave, as I'd said, or go back as soon as the aide had finished bathing him. I tried to concentrate on the decor and ignore the sick feeling in my stomach.

There wasn't much to concentrate on. A few beige plastic chairs, a table with the local weekly, some old *Time* magazines, and several copies of *Reader's Digest Condensed Books* that huddled together for companionship on an otherwise empty shelf.

Fifteen minutes with him, and I feel guilty. Guilty. Small. Little. That's it! Little again!

Unable to sit still any longer, I retraced my steps down the hall, past the nun's desk, and out the door. The sun was warm against my face. I set off down a sidewalk beneath tall trees, walking quickly past small houses with neat exteriors and perfectly tended lawns, not even pausing to enjoy the colorful riot of flowers near their front doors.

I was walking fast, but inside I felt a deep tiredness. It was not yet seven. Everyone would still be sleeping back at the motel. I decided to walk the few blocks to Main Street.

I stepped into a small restaurant. The young waitress was wiping the counter. She looked up and smiled as I opened the door and walked in.

"Mornin'."

"Good morning."

"Have a seat. Anywhere. I'll be right with you."

"I'm just going to have a cup of coffee."

"That's okay. We won't be busy for another hour or so."

She came from behind the counter, drying her hands on her white ruffled apron.

"Black coffee."

"You must be from somewhere else. Of course we serve our coffee black. You have to add the extras."

I smiled, remembering how long and how many ruined cups of coffee it had taken me in New York before I had finally learned to say "*black* coffee." I had always left untouched the whitish, messy-looking brew Manhattanites preferred.

"I used to live here."

Just then, two men in olive-green work clothes, the name of their company embroidered on the pocket, came in. I was grateful for the interruption. I knew from past visits that the waitress, after hearing I lived in New York City, either would be incredulous that anyone could possibly live there or would ask, starry-eyed, about the rich and famous people I might have met.

More likely the first. Colleagues and friends in New York thought that I had improved my life by the choices I'd made, but I knew that most people here thought that I had lost, rather than gained. Here they measured a good life by space, clean air, and an immersion in the beauties and chores of the seasons.

And my father? He'd never recognized any of my accomplishments. Not to me, anyway. No matter what I did, I never felt as if I measured up to my brothers or sisters.

But there had been that one day when, as a young woman, I'd been visiting my parents and my father had asked if I'd drive to Ortonville and pick up a tractor part he'd dropped off for repair. I was happy to do so, and he gave me directions to the implement store.

When I arrived and identified myself, the owner looked at me closely and asked, "You're Roy Hoffbeck's daughter?"

"Yes."

"His youngest daughter?"

"Yes."

"I'm really happy to meet you. He's always talking about you, telling me about your latest accomplishments and adventures."

I nodded but could think of nothing to say because I couldn't meld those two men, that praise-giving man and the man who never told me I'd done anything right.

As pleasant as it had been to hear, that encounter could not erase the image I'd lived with as a girl and young woman. Sitting there in the restaurant that day, facing a familiar huddle of sugar bowl, salt and pepper shakers, and napkin dispenser, I remembered the frustration that overwhelmed me when I was seven and eight. I always hated household chores, and even when I was given work outside the house, the work assigned seemed slight, trivial.

I needed to think things out. If I was going to return to my father, I wanted to be calm, in control of my emotions. As all of us knew, each visit to him might be our last.

I'd go to the river. I hadn't been there since my parents had moved off the farm ten years earlier. I couldn't bear, even now, to see the house, the front porch torn off and the pristine white painted a muddy brown, to see other children in the yard, a different man in the barn, someone else's mother in the kitchen. But I could reach one portion of the river by a back way, from the highway.

I loved that river. It had been recreation, solace, adventure to me. It had also been trouble, work, and fear for all of us. When Joe had visited the farm when we were dating and had seen the meager flow bubbling over and around rocks, he didn't believe my talk of terrible floods. Then I'd pointed to the marks high up on the trees near our house where huge ice chunks had violently gouged permanent reminders of the river's destruction.

I paid the bill, leaving a New York-size tip that widened the eyes of my waitress. I walked quickly back to the motel, found the keys to the Avis car, and left a note. My younger son stirred and opened his eyes. I leaned over him, whispered that I had something important to do and that I'd be back soon. I kissed his forehead as his eyes closed again.

I turned off the highway onto an old gravel road, drove a short way, and parked. I remembered that we had never locked our farmhouse at night, much less a car, but my New York habits would not let me walk away from an unlocked vehicle.

Tall branches of sweet white clover brushed my legs, and the scent made me pause. I inhaled deeply. No other flower's bouquet can compare to the scent of these small, nondescript blossoms that sit along the stem of a rangy plant, progeny of a crop that, at some point, had escaped from a farmer's field.

Tractor ruts were separated by a center strip of grass and weeds. I could feel the large stones through the thin soles of my shoes. I followed this road until I came to a makeshift gate held shut by heavy chain looped over and over. On each side, three strands of barbed wire enclosed the land.

I slipped through the middle and bottom strands of wire. As kids we'd always helped each other through fences and held bushes and tall weeds so that the person following wouldn't be whipped by the branches when they snapped back into place.

Then I looked closely at the twist of the wire, noticed its rusted points, its sharpness. The pain. I remembered the day my father had chased me through a similar fence on our property. Why couldn't he ever have told that little girl she'd done something right? I'd always heard about the others. John's academic achievements. Bill's business acumen. Bob's social ease.

Everything looked blurry. I made myself stop walking. There, across a flat area of short weeds, the river waited, a calm, brassy green. Recent floods had given it a new loop, and the bank was higher. A wide expanse of gray pebbles that had not been there before rooted near the shore. Aliens. Unwelcome and disconcerting. My mind's mental image of the river, unchanged for so many years, was stronger than the reality of what I was actually seeing.

I struggled through tangled brush and came to a small, open area. Ahead I saw a small rivulet, its miniature banks covered with emerald-green grass, running toward the river's edge. I'd come from the opposite direction, but I knew this spot. This was where I had come each summer as a child to look for buttercups. I slipped as I hurried toward it and then bent down to take off my shoes. The mix of rough grasses and weeds hurt my tender feet, but it was cool, and as I neared the tiny stream of water, mud oozed up between my toes. I couldn't find any buttercups.

Moving away from the river, I followed the little stream a short way. Then I saw them. The small, shiny flowers, each petal enameled a vivid yellow, held aloft by slim green stems. I started to pick a few but was forced to pull, then tug, at the stems. I became annoyed at their resilient strength. And then I became annoyed at my own impatience. After all, their strength, not just their beauty, was what they were.

I sat down, then lay back, closing my eyes. Smells of sweet grasses and pungent weeds enveloped me. A bee advanced, its purposeful tiny motor running at top speed, then retreated. A meadowlark praised the morning and the lushness of this one small parcel of land. A breeze wandered through the grass near my head, rattled the leaves on a nearby tree, faded away. The sun soothed my face, comforted my body, dried the mud on my feet, binding my toes together.

There *was* still time, time for the two of us to heal.

I sat up quickly, put my shoes on over my dirty feet, and ran back to the car.

He was lucid today, knew who I was. We would talk. Maybe even laugh. I unlocked the car, backed out the dirt road, and drove fast on the broad, almost deserted highway. The rising sun glinted off the rearview mirror.

Back at the nursing home, I hurried down the hall. I heard strange moans coming from my father's room. Something was wrong.

When he saw me, he cried out, "Myrtle! Quick, get some sandbags! The water's coming up fast!"

I stood, unable to move. My mother's name. He had always called her Mother. Had he reverted during their last, painful years together to calling her by her given name, the two of them once more young sweethearts?

"Oh, God, help me! Don't stand there! Hurry! There's no time! Help me!"

His plea to me echoed mine to God.

I dropped the sprigs of buttercups that I'd brought for him on the dresser near the Christmas tree, went to the door, and closed it. Then I hurried to his bed, took the light blanket at the foot, and rolled it into a tight bundle. I ran to the door and wedged it firmly against the bottom.

My father watched me closely. "The window. Hurry! The water's coming in the window!"

Rushing to the window, I pulled the shade down as far as it would go.

"There's still a space—the water'll come in there!"

Glancing around the room, I saw some towels hanging on the side of the dresser. Quickly I rolled them up, rushed to the window, and filled the space between the shade and the windowsill. Then, catching my breath, I came around the side of the bed, released the rail, and sat beside his thin form.

"We'll be all right now," he said.

I took one of his hands in both of mine and felt his pulse gradually slowing. His face looked foggy to me, and I felt a dampness on my cheeks.

"Do you know who I am?"

I thought of him searching his memories, trying to remember the women in his life. His mother and grandmother, the first of the caring, capable women. His schoolteachers. His brothers' wives. The neighbor women, especially Heinie's wife, Hattie, perhaps pausing to savor her raised doughnuts again. His beautiful, dark-haired daughters, Helen and Patt, and the disappointment that was Dorothy. My mother's gracious sisters, always willing to listen to his stories one more time. His sons' wives, who came into his life, bringing laughter and children again. And, of course, the only woman whose presence or absence really mattered: Myrtle, my mother. Remembering his life with her and maybe unwilling, or unable, to face the rest of his life without her.

"Dad, do you know who I am?"

He smiled.

I waited.

"Of course. The blond one. Barbara."

THE GATE

⌒

The gate is gone. It was never much of a gate. It certainly never kept anyone out. There was no lock. There wasn't even a complete fence to encircle the space within. On the west and the south sides, there was no fence at all. Even when the gate was in place, anyone, any animal—whitetail deer, coyote, stray dog—had equal access.

To enter, you just raised the latch, rusty at its hinges, and pushed forward. The gate would clang back into place after you, the sound ringing in the air for a second or two before joining up with the wind.

Over the years, the road leading to the gate has become increasingly woebegone. Always, still, a person drives over the wooden railroad bridge that my siblings and I crossed on our way to school and takes a left. The road used to be entirely dirt, with wildflowers and weeds fringing its edges, but for the past several years the first quarter mile has been paved to accommodate huge white trucks parked by a foul-smelling cheese plant. Farther along, the original dirt trail is still intact, but on the left, what was once a small, nondescript field is now an informal town dump. And if you look up high into the nonstop blue of a prairie sky, the tower of a huge coal-burning plant diminishes the breadth of the land, and you.

A gate is a portal, a threshold. Lifting the latch and stepping inside are deliberate actions that take you from one place to another. When the gate was in place, that action had left the cheese plant, the dump, even the ugly tower, outside.

How many years have my sister Helen and I opened that gate?

Each summer, certainly for more than twenty years, we've made a pilgrimage to the sacred space. We always go directly to our parents' graves. They're placed side by side, with Dorothy's at their feet. Each year, that walk has become just a little less painful. After our individual silent prayers, with a jumble of memories swirling in and around us, we move on to pay our respects to others.

With no plan, we walk haphazardly from marker to marker. And we always come upon the newest gravesite, its tamped-down earth offering a stark contrast with its neighbors' green grass, and only a metal marker placed upright in the dirt. Grief hits us anew as we see the name of someone we knew and loved when we were children.

We know the family that quarried the granite and the man who polished the stone. And we knew the woman who sketched the scenes on many of the engravings. She, too, now rests below. The people who are buried here knew the people who would craft their lasting memorials. It is all so personal, so intimate.

We never hurry past new gravestones but take time to subtract the first number from the second. Sometimes the total we arrive at is much too low, and we realize, though we've never met these young people, their families are ones we've known, well, forever.

Over time, tradition has evolved. No longer do the gravestones just state the name and dates of birth and death; rather, they've become mini-tableaux of lives lived. Carved into the granite: a guitar for a songwriter; a whirl of flowers for an avid gardener; an elaborate dual farm scene—horses pulling a wagon on one side, a combine moving through a wheat field on the other—for a farmer whose life spanned two centuries.

Helen and I wander, holding our windblown hair back from our faces with one hand. We read. And remember. Sometimes we laugh. More often we dab at our eyes until hazy names become clear again.

At some point, saturated with memories and conflicting emotions, the two of us, without saying a word, walk slowly toward the gate. But the gate is gone. And so this time it's different. There's no way to keep all of that from getting into the car and riding back into town with us.

WILD PLUM COBBLER

In the past when a touchstone was raked across the surface of a rock, the color of the scratch determined the presence—or absence—of gold alloys. Wild plum cobbler is our familial touchstone. My siblings and I are passionate about this esoteric dessert. Others less so. When friends and those who married into our family are presented with a dish of it, they slowly raise the filled spoon to their mouths, and then, with the determination of small children who've been taught to say nice things, pronounce, "Yes, it's good."

Mother's wild plum cobbler brings back to us memories of following one another through fields dotted with wildflowers to the beautiful plum tree. The dessert tugs at our heartstrings in some inexplicable fashion. We loved it when she made an angel food cake from scratch, whipping the thirteen egg whites into a frothy cloud of white, carefully folding in the dry ingredients, and then baking the mixture to a golden brown. And all of us still fondly recall her sweet rolls. Each one was a treat to eye and taste buds: generous swirls of dark cinnamon within the rolls' compact curls, each topped with a dab of not-too-sweet white frosting.

If we'd been thinking of economics—but, of course, we hadn't been—wild plum cobbler would have been at the top of a least-expensive-to-make list, for Mother used slices of bread that she'd baked a day or two earlier in a woodburning stove, cream from our cows, and fruit from the plum tree in our pasture.

The one who spent the fewest years of his life with us on the farm, Bill, became the grand keeper of our family and its traditions. Through the years, as my siblings and I moved away to different states, Bill and his wife, Ruth, made the shift to a suburb northwest of Chicago. The two of them worked hard—though they made it seem easy—to make sure we didn't lose touch with them or with each other. Phone calls, letters, and their open invitation to "come stay with us anytime" kept us all loosely bound.

On one of my visits to Bill and Ruth, at the end of a dinner, where the table was set with fine china and brightened with flowers recently picked from their garden, Bill announced there was to be a surprise. Then he brought in a tray of crystal dishes filled with the family favorite. However, as much as the dessert was appreciated, it had been made with domestic plums, and its flavor proved to be only a proxy of the original. The special tang, the zip, was missing.

One summer when Bill returned to our hometown, he drove down to the farm and, with the permission of the new owners, walked to the pasture where the wild plum tree had flourished. When he reached the site, he found only a bleached brown stump. The plum tree of our memory had died. There was no way to grow a duplicate.

In an attempt to find domesticated plums that would replicate the taste of wild ones, he researched and pored over catalog offerings and, at last, ordered a plum tree. He planted it near the crab apple and fig trees in the mini-orchard he had created at the edge of his large garden. Disappointedly, the tree never yielded more than a few anemically flavored plums. Then John decided to join the search. He found wild plum trees at his wife's childhood farm in Iowa and planted saplings of them in his yard in Indiana. When the word went out that the trees failed to thrive, we were all disappointed.

Over the years, news of my brothers' quest for a fruit-bearing wild plum tree spread beyond our immediate family. Ten years ago, when Bill and Ruth were visiting her hometown, a cousin of a cousin ceremoniously presented Bill with a treasure: three gallons of wild plums from trees that grew eighty miles north of the original bearer of the famed fruit.

Our family reunion had been set in a small town near our farm on the following weekend. Lodging is in short supply in that area—and none of it is grand. The date of our get-together also happened to be the date of two local weddings and a farm-machinery convention. The only reservations we were able to get were at the lowest-rated motel on the local accommodations list.

By the time I'd checked in, I was exhausted. It had been a long day of travel by plane and car. So, after our group returned from a burger-and-fries dinner, I excused myself and went to bed. I was tossing and turning, trying to find a comfortable position on a lumpy mattress, when, sometime before midnight, I heard pounding on my door.

"Barb, meet us in the lobby." I recognized Bob's voice.

"I'm already in bed," I yelled back.

"This is important!" he responded, and before I could even ask what had happened, I heard his voice fading down the hallway as he continued to emphasize that my presence was essential.

I tossed a sweatshirt over my pajamas and grabbed the room key, wondering what could be so pressing.

I hurried down the narrow hallway and walked into an alcove next to the check-in desk. The small space was dominated by a huge soda machine. My sister, three brothers and their wives were crowded together, sitting on folding chairs around a worn Formica table, but Bill was missing.

"What happened?" I asked.

"Just wait," someone said.

A few minutes later, Bill emerged. As he walked in, he mimicked the sound of a trumpet as he held aloft a casserole. The dish was overflowing with wild plum cobbler! He'd baked it at a relative's house and brought it in a cooler.

Then I noticed that a place setting had been set for each of us—a Styrofoam cup and a plastic spoon. The casserole made its rounds. As we served ourselves, trying with the flimsy, shallow spoons to corral the bread and plum sauce into the small cups and keep it from falling onto our clothes, Bill stood behind us and topped each portion of his creation with a dollop of heavy cream.

We all took a bite. A moment of silence, followed by a chorus of "Oh, this is *so* good!"

That was quickly followed by a circle of smiles. Bob jumped up and grabbed more cups and a nearby carafe of coffee and poured some for each of us.

Together we raised our cups, cheered, and thanked Bill for giving us, once again, a taste of our childhood.

LOST

The last time we were all together
Someone said
Remember Mother's wedding ring?
A thin band of white gold
With seven small diamonds.
Mother had seven children.
One child died.
One stone fell out.
Which was lost first?
Child or stone?
None of us had the answer.

ANNUAL PILGRIMAGE

For years, my returns to South Dakota were always trips of necessity. My parents and my parents-in-law endured serial, concurrent medical emergencies. Life-and-death crises intertwined with death itself.

In the middle of the night in Manhattan when the phone clattered from its spot in the kitchen, my chest would tighten as I clambered out of bed and stumbled down the hall to answer it. What had happened? Who had been rushed to the hospital this time? Would it be essential for us to make another long trek back to our hometown with two small children in tow? When my youngest was three and sick with an ear infection, his pediatrician told me I absolutely must not take him on an airplane. I understood the gravity of the doctor's orders, but we had no one to leave my toddler son with. And how could I not say a final goodbye to my mother?

Even if all four of us were well, just getting there was a physical ordeal. The trip involved an often frustratingly slow cab ride to LaGuardia Airport, a three-plus-hour flight to Minneapolis, the hassle of renting and picking up a car from the lot, and then a four-hour drive to our destination.

One time, we made the trip during a terrible ice storm. As we crept along, I prayed and worried. Would we arrive in time for the viewing and recitation of the rosary for my father? We did not, but gratitude that we'd arrived safely helped moderate my disappointment.

After these sad reunions, gathering our belongings and saying goodbye always took longer than anticipated. Following my father's funeral, that had been especially true, and Joe was trying to make up for the lost time on our trip back to the airport. The roads were clear and there was little traffic, so, as we turned onto Highway 7, Joe began driving a few miles above the speed limit. Peter and Stephen sat quietly in the backseat. We were all emotionally drained. Two hours or so into the trip, Peter said he was hungry. Remarkably, in this area of few towns, we spotted a McDonald's on our side of the highway. Convenient indeed.

Joe slowed down and began to pull off. Suddenly the car lurched violently to its right side. Joe turned off the engine. Then he got out. I did the same and helped Peter and Stephen out of the rear passenger door, which was now resting near the ground. We stood silently. None of us could believe what we saw. The rear axle had detached. The car looked like a large broken toy. Peter and Stephen began to cry. Joe and I looked at each other and smiled. We were safe. In my mind, though, I saw the church we'd left two days earlier, four new coffins lined up in front of the altar.

To get to another funeral one winter, we drove through a blizzard at night. As we neared our hometown, the half foot of snow accumulating began to harden into ruts. When Joe inadvertently hit the side of one of them, our car went spinning around in the middle of the highway, crossing over the center line into oncoming traffic. Time was suspended as I watched him fight to keep the car upright and get it back into our lane.

So, years after those nightmare trips had ended and I had an opportunity to make the journey under less traumatic circumstances, it was a relief to pack for one, board the plane solo, open a book, and read my way to the Minneapolis-St. Paul International Airport. I was to represent the college where I worked at a recruitment fair. It was all *so* simple: work for one full day, until noon the next, and then I'd be free for several hours to do as I wished, before I met up with my sister Helen after she left work.

Before takeoff, I looked out the window of the plane and was thankful to see clear skies above, which hinted at an easy flight. Checking the skies comes second nature to me, a habit inherited from my father.

I remembered when I was a child and snow began to fall on our land and the wind picked up, my father would say, "I wonder what kind of blizzard we're in for this time. Well, it'll never be as bad as the Armistice Day blizzard. I'll guarantee you that."

Was that a touch of fear in his voice? As an adult, I happened to be visiting when a terrible blizzard hit. For days it was impossible for us to get into town. Later we learned that a young boy had perished. He'd gone out to his family's barn to feed the animals, but on his return to the house, he'd lost his way.

My mother, who seldom criticized anyone, remarked, "Why didn't his parents tie a clothesline around his waist before sending him out there?" Sorrow and frustration mingled in her words.

Once more, I heard my father intone, "But this was nothing like the Armistice Day blizzard."

I became intrigued with the event that still, all those years later, added that quiver to his voice. So, on the second day after I'd packed up the brochures and the college banner, I took a cab to the Minneapolis library.

I spent the afternoon poring over microfiche replicas of newspapers, reading about horrors and tragedies. The day of that epic blizzard, November 11, 1940, was unseasonably warm in South Dakota and Minnesota. The storm hit unexpectedly and quickly. With no warning and no time, hunters froze to death, shotguns still in their hands. In the fields, herds of cattle were turned into statues of ice. Children, unable to find their way home from school, perished.

Sometime after that, knowing that I was researching the storm, an aunt mailed me her copy of *The Day All Hell Broke Loose*, a compilation of firsthand accounts of people who'd survived the storm. Those details, written and published, some only hours after the monster storm, followed me into the night, into my dreams. One story in particular still haunts me.

FOUND THEM LOCKED TOGETHER, FROZEN AND OTHER STORIES

By W. P. Arndt, D.C.
Sauk Centre, MN

Early that morning my dad and I went six miles up Sauk lake to hunt ducks. The weather wasn't bad but as the day wore on the snow began falling at an alarming rate, so Dad said "Let's pull the decoys and go home."

Two flocks of snow geese had lighted on the lake so I headed the boat into the middle of the lake and the geese. Each flock was reluctant to fly and would simply swim out of the path of the boat. Each time I would raise my shotgun but Dad wouldn't let me shoot on open water. As we approached town we noticed that the lake was so saturated with snow it was just floating slush. When we got into the boat house Dad was sorry we hadn't taken those geese. We could have had a boatload.

When we were back at our house and warm, Dad became concerned about the anti-freeze in his '37 Buick. There was a garage only two blocks up Main street so we tried driving. We wound up with a small Allis Chalmers tractor pulling and several men pushing and shoveling to move the Buick just two blocks. . . . Walking home was something else as we faced that northwest wind. We made it to the mill, out of the wind, and, after catching our breath, we walked backwards about halfway across the bridge to our point of land where the trees blocked enough wind we could stand walking face forward to our house. . . .

Two young brothers, driving a truck, stopped at the

Engle farm southwest of town. Mr. Engle urged them to stay at his place that night because the storm was getting worse and they were lightly clad. They went only a short way and got stuck. They lost their way walking in the storm, following a fence line. The younger brother collapsed first; then the older brother carried him until he could go no further. My uncle, Nolan Gilbert, and some other firemen found them after the storm, locked together, frozen to death.

I've been in other blizzards but this one was the granddaddy of them all.

On that afternoon of research in 1989, I left the Minneapolis library about four o'clock and boarded a bus to the outskirts of the city. Following Helen's instructions, I asked the driver to let me off at County Road 18. Standing by the side of the highway as huge semis whooshed by, I felt ridiculous and vulnerable. What would I do if she didn't come? There were no cell phones then. But, of course, after a fifteen-minute wait, she did. We set off to her small house, which rests on a bank only a few yards above a clear lake.

Early the next morning, we began the drive to our hometown. And with that, our trip to Big Stone City became an annual tradition that we were able to maintain for almost three decades.

During those years, we were witnesses to *change*. We began to notice that once carefully tended houses were no longer maintained. Porch roofs were sagging, and siding had not been refreshed with a new coat of paint. White houses had always been paired with white or red barns. I always thought of the two of them—houses and barns—as partners. And for a few years the barns, always the chief source of pride for farmers, appeared neat as before. Then they, too, became dilapidated. As years passed, Helen and I became transfixed with the bare-bones architecture that was gradually revealed. Later, our fascination turned to alarm as both the houses and the barns disappeared altogether. The fields of single farms had been subsumed into megafields owned by out-of-state companies.

Years later, remembering the sense of loss I felt upon

returning to my hometown, this quote in a review of the book *The Return*, by Hisham Matar, leaped out at me: "What you have left behind has dissolved. Return and you will face the absence or the defacement of what you treasured." And once more I felt anew a sense of loss as I remembered our town's diminished Main Street and those flat fields stripped of their houses and barns.

On that first trip, a few miles before we reached our destination, we were lured by a sign that pointed to an antique store. It was situated on a thriving farm with a large barn and a modern house. Ethel, the woman in charge, had filled the original house with dishes, kitchen utensils, aprons, crystal and china, paintings, photographs, books, and more, much more. When she invited us in, Helen and I stepped into our childhood.

Within the crowded rooms, the spaces between the overladen dressers, tables, and bookcases were narrow. A handwritten sign warned, "If you break it, you buy it." Helen and I looked at each other.

"I'll take our purses to the car," I said. Helen nodded and gave me hers.

Helen and Ethel were about the same age, and soon they set about establishing whom they knew in common. As I browsed, a chorus of "Oh, I didn't know So-and-So married So-and-So's sister!" and "How terrible that he died so young!" followed me as I worked my way room after room.

The first room had originally been a porch; in the process of remodeling—perhaps in the '60s—open spaces had been enclosed with glass. It was light and airy. This room contained paraphernalia that had been essential in the preparation and serving of meals during the first half of the twentieth century. In late afternoon, the low angle of the sun's rays glinted off polished surfaces as I marveled at the variety. I spotted a large Fiestaware bowl, the same size as the one my mother had always used to make bread. This one was blue; hers had been yellow.

The next room held crystal, china, and myriad knickknacks. Sitting on a shelf was a white covered dish in the shape of a hen sitting on her eggs. I have an identical one. It was my Great Aunt Tillie's. She always kept her keys in it.

On one of our trips (of course, stopping at Ethel's became an integral part of that tradition), I found a packet of Christmas cards from the '20s. When I removed the rubber band that held them together and turned over individual ones, I was startled to see that my father's cousin had been the recipient of all of them.

I held the bundle in my hand and hesitated. It had been only a few months since I'd had to empty our country house of all of its furnishings, some of which had been part of my life for decades. The details and colors were exquisite, much finer than those of our contemporary holiday cards. I was torn. Should I buy the entire packet, making it impossible for a stranger to possess any of them? But in doing so I'd be accumulating more things of sentimental value that, in time, I'd have to relinquish. In the end, I selected only three, replaced the rubber band, and reluctantly put the stack back into the basket.

When we quizzed Ethel about her business, she explained that she regularly attended farm and estate sales. With a trained eye, she picked things that she could squeeze into her already stuffed rooms, ones that would appeal to tourists and antique dealers. Her business was a way station where personal treasures from those disappeared farmhouses that Helen and I mourned were transferred to the next generation. Ethel marketed nostalgia.

When Helen and I stepped outside to load our treasures (of course each of us had bought a few things), we paused to admire the farmyard. Grass, mowed and clipped, ran up to the large white house. Tractors and other pieces of farm equipment were parked neatly beside the barn. All was well maintained, all in order. We turned to the view. The shallow valley to the south that began at the edge of the property stretched green for miles, and then we noticed it. There, at the edge of the farmstead, was a silo. The once elegant structure stood roofless, and growing from its open top was a very tall, very spindly box elder tree that reached toward the sky. The silo with a tree growing through its top became a benchmark for us. Year after year, we'd check to see if the silo still stood, if the tree remained green.

And then there was the barn we grew to love. Much as aunts, who have no parental rights and therefore must remain silent, root for their nieces and nephews to succeed, to keep going despite setbacks, we rooted for this barn. It was very old, built of exceptionally wide boards, and showed no sign that it had ever been painted. It snuggled into a small scoop of the otherwise flat terrain. We watched in very slow motion—these were annual trips, after all—as it began to list a few feet off plumb. Each successive trip, we could not deny the fact that it was slipping farther and farther. Then one year, with alarm, we saw that someone had stripped the barn of its beautiful oversize siding. Shingles on the roof had been blown off long ago by harsh north winds. It had continued to stand through blizzards and hailstorms. It was just an outline now. But posts still held up beams, rafters still rose to the ridgeline. It was naked and it was beautiful—a work of art. It became the Skeleton Barn.

It had been built well. It continued to stand. Each year, as we approached the highway curve that would swoop down to allow a view, we'd ask, "Do you think the Skeleton Barn is still standing?"

Each time we were relieved, until 2012, that is. When we rounded the curve and looked down, we saw only a mass of debris.

Helen and I, daughters of a farmer, compulsively inspected the crops beside the road as we drove along. We'd note the results of too much rain: corn leaves yellow, stalks short; too little rain: the leaves not a vibrant green but rather brownish and curled at the edges. We'd empathize with and admonish the owners, "Harvest that wheat, now. You'll lose it all if a strong wind hits."

And, with regret, we saw the changes in the kinds of crops that were grown. It was no longer profitable to grow flax, and I was disheartened when I realized that never again would I see huge fields of uninterrupted azure when the grain blossomed. Later, some of those fields were planted with sunflowers, but, though the vivid yellow of their large blossoms offered some solace, it seemed a meager consolation prize.

For miles and miles, gangly irrigation pipes began to be suspended above the fields, adding an unwelcome mechanical element to the verdant scene. No longer were there unimpeded views of nature where crops met sky.

The small towns changed also: family-owned stores closed, fast-food chains moved in, FOR SALE signs appeared on front lawns, parishes reverted to mission status, populations shrank.

And, of course, the cemeteries grew.

CARTING GOOSEBERRIES
AND CHANDELIERS

~

In a large part of the United States, from Chicago westward through Minnesota and the Dakotas, people are busy carting treasured items from one household to another. About fifteen years ago, after a trip back to visit old friends and members of my scattered family, I came away with a vision of people in continual movement, like ants, carrying things to one another. In my mind's eye, I see families opening car doors and trunks, carefully placing packages within, arriving at doorways with jars of newly preserved fruits and vegetables, handing over bundles of newspapers with green sprigs poking out.

No one met anyone without handing over some *thing*. These were not hostess gifts as we think of them in the East. There was no feeling of obligation on the part of the giver, and many of these were given not by guest to hostess but rather from hostess to guest. On that journey, from the suburbs of Chicago to my hometown, I saw this sharing of abundance. In some cases, it was a casting-off of what one person didn't want to someone who seemed to want it desperately.

At my brother Bill's house, before we drove over to visit his daughter, this custom required that Bill use a hand truck to haul a large pot of thriving mint from the patio to the driveway. Then, using two-by-fours, he improvised a ramp with which to load the mint into the car. Arrival at my niece's home included, of course, the challenge of removing the forty-pound tub of earth and fragrance from the trunk.

Before I left Bill's, my sister-in-law Ruth gave me a small book of her family's favorite recipes and sayings. Also a T-shirt that announced in bold colors, IF AGING IMPROVES THINGS, I'M APPROACHING MAGNIFICENCE!

My next stop was Minneapolis, where my lifelong friend Josie greeted me at the airport. We met the first day of first grade at the only school in our small town and have been remeeting in real cities around the world ever since—from Minneapolis to Milwaukee, San Francisco to Boston, Tehran to Beirut.

We picked up my sister Helen at her home near Annandale, northwest of Minneapolis. There, Helen presented me with a set of three old mixing bowls she had found, one blue, one green, one yellow. Helen had found a yellow bowl identical to one our mother had used! She'd keep her eyes open for the fourth in the set, red. She also gave me a shirt of fine white cotton with pleats down the front from her closet to shield me from the summer sun.

Our destination, of course, was Big Stone City. It takes a great deal of emotional courage to return to that spot where we grew up. The state of current agricultural economics has taken its toll. Like many small towns, Big Stone has lost banks and businesses. The lumberyard is closed now, and the old building that housed the grocery store stands empty and neglected. The main street reminds me of an old mouth, smiling, with several teeth missing. And, of course, there are more personal losses as well. The people we pay our respects to in the cemetery now number more than those we visit in their homes. Making the trip with people you love helps.

My brother John and his wife arrived shortly after we did. Following dinner that night, John announced that he had something for Helen. He pulled his car up next to Josie's. Then, in the motel parking lot, a full moon enhancing the dim wattage of the outdoor lights, we made room in the trunk of Josie's car for a strangely shaped cast-iron piece, some three feet across. Found in the attic of a niece's new house in Glen Ellyn, Illinois, the best guess was that it was a part of an old ceiling fan. In the backseat, we carefully secured a 1920s brass-and-porcelain chandelier from the receiver of the mint's house in River Forest, Illinois. These two items had traveled the farthest and still had more than a hundred miles to go. From Illinois they'd been carted to John's house in Indiana, then through Iowa into mid-eastern South Dakota, where John attended his class reunion, and on up to Big Stone City to link up with Helen and a ride to her little antique shop.

With that accomplished, John announced that he had brought something for me. I was happy to see that the package was small. When I opened it, I found a mug from his class reunion (we share the same alma mater). It fit neatly into the glove compartment.

The next day, we visited relatives and friends and took a long, thoughtful walk through the cemetery. Before we left town, we stopped at the house where Josie grew up. Her brother lives there now. With his blessing, we dug ferns from his garden for Josie to plant in hers. Wrapping the roots carefully to keep them moist, we tucked the plants between the chandelier's arms. We also gathered rhubarb, selecting young stalks with a perfect ratio of red to green.

And we packed gooseberries. A two-gallon bucket of gooseberries. Only if you have picked gooseberries can you appreciate that amount. All three of us picked these in Josie's sister-in-law's garden. Helen said picking those berries was the highlight of her visit. As children we picked wild gooseberries, few larger than a pea, from thorn-filled branches amid clouds of mosquitoes on hot July days in spots where there never seemed to be a breeze. Two of us could pick for hours and return home with only a quart of the hard little whiskered berries. In this lush garden in Big Stone City, with a view of the beautiful lake a few hundred yards away, we would lift a long branch of the tall hybrid bushes and see berries hanging down like bunches of grapes. They were large, easy to grasp by the handful, and they'd plunk, noisily, satisfyingly, into the bucket. More than one berry measured an inch across.

By the time the three of us piled into Josie's Honda to make the return journey from Big Stone City to Minneapolis, the trunk was stuffed with our luggage and the mystery piece of cast iron. Into the last available nook, we put the paper bag containing the rhubarb. We struggled to keep enough room for Helen in the backseat, where we placed the bucket of gooseberries on the floor beneath the chandelier. Heading east, we sometimes hit rough spots on the highway. Then the chandelier chimed gently and the lacy green stems of the fern waved at the window.

Following their air-conditioned ride, the gooseberries arrived in Josie's kitchen, where, after hours of work (there is only one way to remove those whiskers, and that is berry by berry), she made wonderful tart-sweet gooseberry jam.

Of course I carted my accumulated treasures back to New York. The set of mixing bowls and the college mug, I had packed and shipped. I put the white shirt, the T-shirt, and the book of recipes in my suitcase. And in my backpack, along with my journal and writing, I placed a small jar of Josie's gooseberry jam.

Too soon I was back at my regular life and work. During one of those hot, muggy July days in New York, I wasn't feeling well. I left work early with a terrible headache. The apartment was quiet and cool, easy on my pounding head. I went to the kitchen and put on some water for tea, then opened the refrigerator. There was the jar of Josie's creation. Plugging in the toaster, I made some whole-wheat toast and slathered on the gooseberry jam.

FINAL DETAILS

⌐

The weatherman had been right. In Manhattan, rain had turned to sleet. Bits of ice *ping-ping*ed on my umbrella, and I saw that the sidewalk was beginning to freeze over. I chose my steps carefully as I walked two blocks to meet my friend Diana. When I'd heard the revised forecast that morning, I'd suggested to her that we postpone the meeting, but Diana wouldn't hear of it.

"You need to get this done and over with," she said.

Oh well—the weather fit the task ahead. Both were going to present challenges. After some time, we managed to hail a cab and slip and slide our way to its door. It was a slow ride the twelve blocks to the funeral home, but we were only a few minutes late for my appointment.

We were escorted into a large office with lots of dark wood and introduced to Skip, our assigned counselor. After I was queried and answered a lot of questions, Skip took us to a lower level and showed us into a room crowded with rows and rows of caskets.

"This is one of our most popular models," Skip said. "It's simple, with a recessed carrying ledge. That way, there's no need for a lot of hardware."

"The wood is mahogany," he continued, pointing to a glossy deep brown—almost black—model.

I didn't respond, and Diana, standing by my side, was quiet also. No sounds from outside, either. We were in a well-lit, well-cushioned room one level below the street.

"Now, that one is also a popular model," Skip continued, pointing to another sample. "It's walnut."

Joe and I had just stepped into our seventies, and his health was in rapid decline. I was doing this—preplanning, it's called—because I didn't want my sons to experience what we'd had to do a lifetime earlier when Joe's mother had passed away.

Those many years before, we'd flown from LaGuardia to Minneapolis with Peter, four years old, and Stephen, just a year old. We rented a car at the airport and then drove four hours west to Big Stone City.

There, we greeted and tried to comfort Joe's father, a hollowed-out version of the man we knew. And we learned that we had to choose a casket for my mother-in-law that very evening. Somehow I found a woman willing to sit with the boys. Then Joe and I drove another fifteen miles, arriving late in the evening at the funeral home, which had been reopened just for us. Exhausted and grieving, we entered, met the director, and did our best to choose a casket that my mother-in-law, a perfectionist, would have approved of.

Here in New York, in the room near Madison Avenue, Skip was waiting for my reaction. The walnut sample looked faded, without character.

"What about this one?" I said, pointing to one in the corner.

"Oh, that's smaller. Jewish cemeteries often require a smaller size."

"I like this wood more. But would it be large enough?"

"Is your husband a large man?"

"No. We're about the same size."

"Diana, would I look crowded in there?"

A look of dismay crossed her face. I knew what had happened. She'd been keeping her emotional distance, viewing this as an exercise for Joe, not me. But, of course, we both knew that I'd be doing this only once.

"No, you would fit." After a pause, she added, "Comfortably." She tried to smile.

"I'll leave you alone for a few minutes," Skip said.

"I know none of this really matters," I said to Diana, "but I don't like any of them. That one looks like a supersized men's patent leather shoe, and that one looks like it's been standing out in the sun and rain for a month. And the small one . . . At the service it may look . . . Oh, I don't know—minimal, inconsequential. Maybe the point is that I shouldn't like them."

"Any decision?" Skip was back.

"Barbara doesn't care for these," Diana told him. "Perhaps you have some others?"

"Oh, we do. Come with me." He led us to another room. "These are our less expensive models."

Diana and I gave each other a look. I walked to the far corner. "I like this one. Look at the beautiful grain! You couldn't see the grain on the others."

I turned to Skip. "My husband worked with wood. Both of our sons do also. We all love wood."

I thought of the hours Joe and I had spent choosing just the right woods when we designed our house: Douglas fir for the soaring beams, cherry for the kitchen cabinets, wide-board red oak for the floors, quarter-sawn white oak for the dressing room cabinets. Each piece of wood, and its finish, used in building our house had been chosen with deliberate and loving care. And, of course, the same was true for each piece of furniture.

Our love extends even more to trees. Our house was sited in the midst of trees. Arborists were amazed at the numerous varieties of hardwoods and pines on our property. Joe and I fought to keep as many of those trees as possible as the drive was laid out and the house was built. We were heartbroken each time another tree had to be felled by a chain saw.

During that time, I had to undergo a medical test in which I was slid headfirst into a narrow, completely enclosed, stainless-steel tunnel. The technician warned me if I accidentally touched its edge, the test would be invalid and have to be repeated. I dared not move, he told me, not even a millimeter.

In the tunnel, in total darkness, I searched my mind for something to concentrate on. I began to list the kinds of trees in our woods. Then I began to arrange them alphabetically.

"Apple, ash, aspen, cedar, cherry, cottonwood . . ."

If I remembered another tree as I went along, I couldn't just add it but made myself start over from the beginning. My self-imposed rules required that the finished list be in perfect alphabetical order.

The medical test went on and on. At last, I was rolled out of the tube. I let out a long breath. However, my relief was short-lived.

"We have to put you back in again," the technician announced nonchalantly.

"I'm not sure I can do it."

"Oh, it won't be as long this time."

Back into the narrow darkness. I began to feel claustrophobic. How could I possibly hold still?

I started my list again, but that didn't seem to work. I realized I needed to make the rules of the game harder. So, as I listed the trees, I added the separate species. In alpha order, of course.

Apple; ash; aspen (big tooth, quaking); birch; cherry; cottonwood; dogwood (gray, pagoda, red); elm (American, slippery); on through to several species of maple and to the oaks (black, chestnut, pin, red, white); and then all the way on to walnut, willow, witch hazel.

Years later, even knowing that those trees now belong to someone else, in times of stress when all I can do is sit still and wait for news—good or bad—I begin, "Apple, ash, aspen . . ."

In the tomb-like silence, Diana and Skip waited for my response.

"I like the finish of these much better than those in the other room," I said.

"Those had high-gloss finishes. These are satin."

"Oh. We never used high gloss when we painted," I said. "I like this one. The grain is beautiful."

"It's poplar," Skip said.

"That's appropriate," I replied. "Poplar is in the cotton-wood family. We grew up with cottonwoods. And look how beautifully the grain of the door matches the box itself."

"Of course. It's cut from a single piece of wood," Skip said.

"This one. This is it. Can you make sure the grain matches?"

"Of course. I'll specify that."

And so our contracts state:

To be cut from one piece of wood. Grain must match.

TRAVELING WITH BOB

⌐～

The trip had been a mistake, it seemed. I was going to be forced to sleep overnight in the back of a van or stay in a cabin with no plumbing and risk meeting a bear, black or grizzly, or both, while on a middle-of-the-night trek to essential facilities.

The phone call had been completely unexpected. Even more so was the opening sentence, "Barb, how'd you like to go to Alaska?"

Bob's voice in North Dakota boomed over the phone, sounding as though he were shouting at me from the end of my hallway.

"Why are you asking?"

And then Bob told me of his plans. He was going to drive from his home in eastern North Dakota through the Canadian Rockies to Alaska.

"I need to know by next week," he said.

"What? Why so soon?"

"Well, if you're coming, I'll plan my trip around your arrival, swing over to Anchorage to pick you up."

It was a time when I was feeling particularly fragile. In my sixties, I'd recently nursed my family through a string of medical crises. Bob, I suspected, was feeling freshly invigorated after hearing good news following a cancer episode. And I'd always wanted to visit Alaska.

"It'll be the end of the season. Are you sure we'll be able to get reservations?"

"Reservations? Hell. I'm driving my '84 Dodge Caravan. If we get stuck, we'll just sleep in the truck. I'll throw in a sleeping bag for you."

His mission was to see a grizzly. Preferably up close.

"Can we go to Homer?"

"Homer? I've never heard of it. What's so special about Homer?"

"If I go, I'll explain."

I put Bob's offer on hold for a few days. Two of my friends who had brothers, brothers who would never make such an offer, thought I must go. They saw it as an unparalleled opportunity. But our siblings weren't so sure.

Bill thought it was ridiculous. "You don't know what the weather will be. You might get trapped up there in a blizzard."

John said only, "Well, I don't know . . . ," and then his voice trailed off.

"How long will the trip be?" our sister Helen asked me.

"Two weeks."

There was a long pause as I held the receiver. Finally she said, "Two weeks is a long time."

Roughing it gave me pause. I'm a planner. And searching for bears definitely was not my style. But more than that: Would Bob and I get along? Only two years apart in age, we'd been inseparable as kids growing up. But it had been forty years since we'd spent more than a few hours together at a time, and in those ensuing decades we'd lived more than a thousand miles apart and grown even further apart in our views. The environment, gun control, political parties—name an issue, we sit at opposite poles. Talk about red and blue. And the 2004 presidential election was only weeks away.

At the last minute, I told Bob I'd meet him in Anchorage and shipped my parka and long underwear on ahead.

Not able to accept the possibility of no bed on the very first night, I made reservations at a bed-and-breakfast in Anchorage. And because my only must-do in Alaska was to stay in Homer, on the water, I made reservations there also.

"Why Homer?" Bob asked. "I've never heard of bear sightings in those parts."

I told him about Annie. She and I had worked in different departments at a small college in Manhattan. One particular day, every person we'd dealt with had been difficult or impossible. I'd seen a PBS special the night before about Homer; it had shown moose wandering the streets and snowcapped mountains reflected in the clear waters of the bay. From my sofa in Manhattan, I saw Homer as a pristine paradise at the end of the United States.

"We'll just have to go to Homer," I told Annie. And so "Homer" became our mantra. On overworked and discouraging days, we'd say, "Homer," and smile.

Then Annie received a diagnosis of breast cancer. She took control, timing her chemotherapy and radiation treatments so that she was able to keep on working. She fought for her life, and won. For a time. Two years later, the cancer came back with a vengeance. I didn't even get a chance to say goodbye. Now, I had to visit Homer. For Annie.

Bob was waiting at the Anchorage airport.

"I did a test-drive last night," he told me. "I didn't want you to have to wait."

I thanked him. Although he'd been sitting quite a while, he seemed out of breath.

"On my drive through the Canadian Rockies and British Columbia, I saw so much beauty! I'd see a spectacular mountain, think there couldn't be anything more beautiful, and then the next day there'd be another. Unbelievable! Each day the views were better than the day before!"

He was almost hyperventilating.

That evening, before we retired to our separate rooms, I brought up something that had been on my mind since I'd agreed to go on this trip.

"Bob, can we agree that politics and anything remotely related to it will be off-limits?"

"What fun is there in that?" he countered.

"Please," I drew the word out.

"Oh, okay, if that'll make you happy."

"There's one more thing," I said.

"And what's that?"

"No dirty stories."

"Now, why would you ask for that?" Bob responded.

"You're good at telling them, I admit. And I do laugh at a few. But sometimes you go too far and the stories make me uncomfortable."

"Hmm . . ."

I didn't push him. And he didn't say any more.

Homer was to be our first destination. But while Bob and I were spreading generous layers of native-berry jam onto home-made scones, enjoying our first Alaskan breakfast, the owner told us that if we wanted to see wildlife in Denali National Park, a four-hour drive, we had to head there right away. Winter was coming in fast, and the authorities were about to shut down the buses, the only way tourists are allowed to venture into the interior. Seeing wildlife (read: bears) was paramount to Bob.

We looked at each other and nodded. I called the inn in Homer and changed our arrival date; Bob checked the park bus schedules. We tossed our luggage into the van and headed out.

When we reached the Anchorage city limits, I pulled out the map, preparing to navigate.

"What are you *doing*?" Bob asked.

"Keeping us on the right road," I said.

"Put that map down! Look out! Just enjoy all that beauty!"

It began to snow before we reached the park, and when we arrived, we found that bus service had been suspended for the day. The snow continued to fall lightly. Heavier snow was forecast. We drove, both of us on the lookout for bears, until we reached a Do Not Enter barricade. Bob turned around, and we drove the loop again. No luck. Then Bob said he thought we should leave, abandoning the opportunity to go farther into the park the next day and forgoing lodging near the park. He was worried about getting trapped in a blizzard. I trusted his judgment—he lives in North Dakota, after all—and so we headed out.

We drove and drove, making one stop for gas and "dinner": two granola bars, and a Snickers for dessert. It's not as though there were no rooms—there were no *motels*. At last, we found an open motel with one available room. A bed for me. A cot for Bob.

As we waited for the night clerk to complete our reservation, Bob said, "Barb, look to your left."

I did and was startled by a huge taxidermied grizzly towering above me.

"That's a beauty!" Bob said to the clerk. "How tall is he?"

"Oh, just a little over nine feet," the clerk replied.

Before I fell asleep, I tallied up. We'd changed our plans three times. And that was only day one.

The next day, backtracking, we headed to Homer. On the side of the road, we read a sign that proclaimed, HOPE.

"Do you want to go to Hope?" Bob asked.

We had one no-reservation night before we'd reach Homer. "I don't know."

Bob looked at me over his dark glasses.

"Barb, if you don't go to Hope now, you never will," he said, already signaling and slowing down to take the turn.

The road began as tarmac, then turned to gravel. It was almost twilight, time to find a room in this town of 270 residents. There was only one restaurant, which would be closing in a short time. We decided we'd have a quick dinner and then look for lodging. Bob talks to everyone, and soon patrons and waitresses were telling of their recent encounters with grizzlies and other bears. As the stories multiplied, I grew anxious. I wanted to sleep in a bed, within walls. I paid the bill and headed for the door. Bob was encouraging the storytellers, and their stories were getting better, or worse, depending on your viewpoint.

"Bob. Bob. *Bob!*"

He stood and, with his head turned so as not to miss a word, sidestepped his way to the door.

Climbing into the van, we set off to search for lodging. We turned at a sign that read, Rooms. Under the tall pines, the light of day had begun to dim. We stood near a small cabin twenty yards from a rushing stream. An idyllic location.

A middle-aged woman with a did-it-herself haircut stepped out.

"Do you have a room available tonight?" Bob asked.

"Yes, I have a cabin with two beds."

"Showers?"

"Yes, the toilets and showers are over there," the owner said, pointing toward a small building a city block away.

"This is great! Have you seen any bears this week?" Bob asked.

The tone in his voice let me know he'd actually like to meet a bear on the way to the john at night. This was what I'd been afraid of. Now we'd disagree and begin to argue, one of us would have to give in, and resentment would color the rest of our trip.

"Bob," I said, "I don't think I can do it."

"No?" He tried for neutral but couldn't hide his disappointment.

"No."

Shrugging, he asked the woman about other lodging possibilities. She knew every place around but didn't think there were any vacancies.

"Perhaps we could ask the people back at the restaurant?" I said to Bob.

We headed back to our new friends. The regulars deliberated, and the owner called around. She found a place with one bed and a cot. The lodging, above a convenience store, was run by a hunting guide who supplied not only a key to the room but also directions to a bear-viewing mountain road. We didn't unload our luggage but headed out immediately. We drove until dark. No luck.

At the restaurant the next morning, we were again fed well, both with food and with stories. As we were leaving, I asked the cashier if there was a place where I could buy local crafts. She told me of one, and Bob agreed to delay our trip by fifteen minutes. We easily found the log cabin she'd described; the town consisted of only twenty buildings.

Stepping inside, I was amazed to see a great assortment of items—bowls, boxes, walking sticks—all hand-carved out of wood harvested from local fallen trees. As I looked at each one, Danny, the shopkeeper, named the tree species of the item. Ash, poplar, cedar. I was the only customer, and he was happy to answer my questions.

"Are all of these carved by Native Americans?" I asked.

"Yes. I carved many myself. But we don't use that term here," he said.

"What do you prefer?" I asked.

"'Native Alaskan,'" he answered, "It refers to all the indigenous peoples of Alaska."

While I'd been shopping, Bob had been waiting in the van. He'd picked up a local flyer as we'd left the restaurant and was perusing ads for property in the area. When I returned to the van, there was excitement in his voice. More than usual.

"Barb, look at these prices! They're just crazy. Land is cheap up here! I'm coming back next year and buying a few acres. Build a cabin. Nothing fancy. There'll be no running water, but the streams are so clean, that won't be a problem."

He continued talking as he started the engine and headed out to the main road.

It was hard to leave Hope, but Homer beckoned. We drove there and did stay on the water. As we dined, sea otters cavorting only a few yards from our table entertained us. As dusk approached, we hurried through our meal and then drove to another beach, where we stayed until the sun went down, looking for special stones, including green jade.

The next day, the main thoroughfare was busy with townspeople and tourists. We joined a group waiting in line for a boat trip to neighboring islands. On the ride, we were excited when we saw a whale breech and a bald eagle swoop down to catch a fish, but when we returned to the dock, we found Homer's commercial attractions distracting, compared with the boat trip and its focus on natural history.

I now realize Hope was my Homer. Hope was a small, peaceful town populated with caring people. A place that renewed my spirit.

The rhythm of the trip was set during those first days. We didn't have a schedule of any sort. We only had to make it to Vancouver in time for my return flight.

And so we drove through the Kenai Peninsula, and the Yukon, into British Columbia and on through the Cassiar Mountains. We called out, "Look at that glacier! Look at the snowcapped mountains! Look at those red leaves! Look at the moose! Look at that incredible view of the river! Look at that waterfall!"

And, also, "Bob! Look at the road!"

We had planned at the end of the trip to catch a ferry between Haines, Alaska, and Bellingham, Washington, a short drive from the Vancouver airport, which would have saved us about 1,500 miles of driving. But we learned that one ferry was out of service and the others were fully booked. So, with a lot of miles to cover, we made the most of our long days. We stopped to take photos of scenery and of signs (my favorite: MOOSE RUT-TING, NEXT 5 MILES) and, of course, for gas and coffee, but enthusiasm was our main fuel. We never turned on the radio, and I never looked at a map while we were moving again. There was so much to see that I didn't plan to miss any of it. We needed nothing more than the views outside the van's windows.

The trip was a revelation—not only thanks to Alaska's unparalleled, breathtaking beauty, but also because of what I learned about my brother.

For a man who revels in his second career, working as a predator controller, which means stalking wildcats in the mountains of Texas, he was, to my surprise, exceedingly thoughtful.

For me, the day begins only after I've had a cup of coffee. Because the places we stayed had minimal amenities in the off-season, that cup was often hard to come by. Every morning, as soon as he got up, Bob would toss on his leather jacket and head out the door. Soon he'd be back, handing me a large Styrofoam cup of steaming coffee.

At the farthest northern reaches of our trip, the edges of glaciers, permafrost beneath our feet, we found that almost all businesses were closed. We traveled with bags of nuts. Without saying a word, Bob would hold out his palm. I'd tip the bag into his waiting hand. We had to keep moving.

If gas stations were scarce, toilet facilities were almost non-existent. When we did find a place to gas up, I'd always ask about a restroom. One time, the attendant didn't speak, only pointed to an add-on at the side. Not knowing what to expect, I cautiously opened the door. There *was* a toilet. That was a relief. I thought there might be only a hole in the floor, as I had often found to be the case during my travels in Asia. But as I stepped forward, the floorboards moved down. Between the gap my weight had created, I could see the ground below. Without turning, I stepped slowly back. Bob was still at the pumps. Talking.

"I'm afraid I'm going to fall right through the floor in there," I said. "You're heavier than I am. Will you test it out?"

He raised his eyebrows, hesitated a moment, and then did as I asked.

Bob quizzed everyone we met, trying to satisfy his innate curiosity and to advance his goal of seeing a grizzly. We chose our routes on the basis of where the chances for that would be best.

One day, as the sunlight faded and I became ever more concerned about finding lodging for the night, we drove into Glennallen. The town, according to the last census, was situated in an "unorganized borough," population 483.

We stopped at the only place that wasn't closed for the season. A handwritten sign was taped on the door: "Attention, all guests: Please be advised that there has been a bear behind the hotel. Do not walk behind the hotel. Beware of your surroundings. Thank you!"

When we entered our dilapidated room, the only one available, we looked out the window and saw a young couple setting up a pup tent on the other side of the hotel's wire fence.

"Look at that great bear bait," Bob said, referring to the young man and woman. "I'm sure to spot at least one bear tonight."

"Bob, go out and warn them. They didn't check into the motel. They couldn't have seen the sign. They don't know about the bears!"

"But they'll have a great vantage point to see one," he said, as he slowly—for my benefit—picked up his jacket and headed to the door.

It was dark when we returned from dinner, so I wasn't able to check on the young couple, but in the morning I was relieved that there was no sign of them or their belongings. Bob was disappointed that he hadn't scored a sighting.

It seems strange now, but gift shops became an entry point for me to learn about the native culture. I was astonished at how many ways contemporary artists have refined and integrated ancient designs and symbols into their work. My questions about the items and my appreciation of their beauty elicited detailed explanations from the clerks and artisans.

Bob, who good-naturedly grumped whenever I asked him to stop, declaring that we were wasting precious driving time, also took advantage of the breaks by standing outside the shops and talking to anyone who passed by.

I'd been successful in tamping down Bob's jokes as we rode along thousands of miles and shared numerous meals. Until one day in British Columbia. I wanted to buy a small object, an old one, for Helen, but, though I'd been on the lookout, I hadn't seen any establishment advertising antiques. A waitress told us to watch for a SECONDHAND sign and gave us directions.

As I entered the barnlike structure, I smelled a combination of furniture polish and tea. Everything was organized by category and era. I was pleased when I found two old, red-handled kitchen utensils to add to Helen's collection. The owner offered to box them up. As she did so, we chatted. When I told her I lived in Manhattan, she offered sympathy, referencing 9/11. Then she began to tell the sad story of her son's death. He'd gone in for a routine checkup. At the end of the visit, with no one there to support him, the young man had learned he had only three months to live. The woman said her greatest regret was not having been there with her son; he was forced to hear the news alone. I did my best to offer my condolences.

In the meantime, Bob had settled into an easy chair next to the owner's husband. I couldn't understand his words, but I could tell from the rhythm of Bob's voice that he was telling one of his stories.

I picked up my box and headed for the door. Without breaking the rhythm of his story, Bob waved me on.

"Were you telling one of your dirty jokes?" I snapped when he climbed into the van.

"Yep."

"Do you know that the woman and her husband just lost their son?"

"No, I didn't," he said, taking a moment to look over at me, "but when I left she was laughing more loudly than her husband. And I think, given what you just told me, that was a good thing for both of them."

I had to admit he was right.

Farther along in British Columbia, we detoured in order to drive through a réserve, a clearly delineated territory deeded to the indigenous people.

A large sign warned us that if we continued we'd be subject to the laws of the First Nations, and, would be prosecuted under tribal laws. On another day at 'Ksan, a reconstructed village, we were frustrated that we couldn't stay longer so we could learn more about the indigenous culture and the injustices those people had suffered.

Bob and I both recognized the irony of this. As adults traveling thousands of miles away from home, we were eager to learn, but while growing up we'd had no knowledge of the lives of the Dakota Sioux who resided on a reservation only sixty miles from our farm.

A day later, we discovered crucial bear information when I was the one to initiate a conversation. For hours we'd driven in heavy rain and fog through mountains on a narrow dirt road. We decided to stop for coffee to calm our nerves. We were at a junction, about to head toward Prince Rupert, leaving bear country. While Bob was at the gas pump, I went into the small store, ordered two cups of coffee, and sat down. The woman in the next booth was an Alaskan resident. I told her of Bob's disappointment in not having found a bear. If we wanted to see bears, she said, we'd have to change directions and go to Hyder. The salmon were running.

I thanked her. As we set out, Bob turned toward Stewart. It was dark and raining when we arrived. Stewart is in British Columbia, Hyder is in the United States, yet the two towns are only a few miles away from each other. Our motel was in Stewart. The bears were in Alaska. We crossed the border several times during our short stay between the two countries, the boundary marked only by a wooden bridge and a border guard.

The afternoon of our first full day there, we stopped at a shop near that bridge. It featured beautiful handcrafted jewelry side by side with gleaming, efficient-looking hunting knives. The owner, who looked as though he could take care of himself in any situation, explained the different salmon runs and with that information gave us the key to what times of the day and where to look for bears.

As we were about to leave, he offered another bit of advice: "Keep in mind that grizzlies may look clumsy, but they're fast-moving critters!"

At twilight, we followed the shopkeeper's directions, and— at last—we spotted a young black bear and two older blacks wandering down the middle of the road.

"Well, Bob, you've seen your bear! And more than one!" I said.

"Yes, but not a grizzly." Disappointment was heavy in his voice.

We continued on, even though the road was becoming narrower and rockier. In some places, it disintegrated into a slough of muddy water.

And then, on Bob's side of the van, across the narrow stream, there was a grizzly! As though posing for us, he held and was chomping upon a large salmon.

The bear was on the other side of the stream. The narrow road, which had no shoulder, dropped right down into the rushing water. The distance wasn't great, but, I reasoned, the bear was preoccupied. And the scene would make a perfect photo. I opened the door, hurried to the front of the van, and began to focus my camera. Then, through the viewfinder, I saw that the bear had stopped munching and was looking directly at me!

Common sense returned in a flash. I turned around and ran back to the van. Bob had already leaned over to push my door wide open.

THINKING ABOUT BEANS

〜

M y mother made her baked beans three times a year: at
Thanksgiving, at Christmas, and for the annual Farmers'
Day picnic in July. I remember helping her when I was a child.
She'd spread the beans out on a baking tin, and together we
would carefully check to make sure that there were no bean-size,
bean-colored stones among them. After soaking and boiling the
beans, she'd scoop one out with a long-handled spoon. Then
she'd blow on the bean to cool it and, holding it between her
forefinger and thumb, slip the outer skin off.

"This is how you test the beans," she said.

Years later, at Christmas, when I returned to visit my
parents in their farmhouse in South Dakota, my husband experienced my mother's baked beans for the first time—mahogany
in color, each bean separate but melded together by a smoky,
sweet, what-is-that? flavor. He ate the first serving and asked
for seconds, then thirds. And I asked my mother for the recipe.

A few years later, Joe and I traveled to Europe. High on
our list of must-see places was Carcassonne, the medieval walled
city in southern France. The best cassoulet in the world, a main
dish whose primary ingredient is beans, is purportedly made

in Carcassonne. Joe diligently researched restaurants and then made reservations at the one known to serve the premier cassoulet in Carcassonne. Now, we're talking about the Mouton Rothschild of cassoulets and, perhaps, of beandom itself.

For me, tasting beans prepared the French way in France was slightly short of momentous. As the family story goes, our bean recipe was of French origin, having migrated in the mid–eighteenth century with my maternal ancestors—maybe, I like to think, tucked in the corner of an old wooden trunk, but more likely in the corner of a woman's mind. Those ancestors left a small town in France for Québec, Canada, where at least one of them, a young man, fought under Marquis de Montcalm. From there, many years later, a variation of the bean recipe traveled with my great-grandmother to Pierre, South Dakota.

That evening in the best-cassoulet-in-Carcassonne restaurant, Joe and I scanned the menu and, of course, ordered what we'd come for. We waited. A large, covered crock was brought to our table and the lid removed with great ceremony. Eagerly, we spooned portions onto our plates. We took one taste. No smiles. No "aha" moment.

"Your mother's beans are better," Joe said.

My mother always slow-cooked her beans in the oven (for many years in a wood-fired stove, then, later, in a gas stove) while she prepared them for the three ceremonial feasts. Because the small oven in my Manhattan apartment could hold only beans or a bird, I didn't attempt to make them for decades after my mother had died, long after we'd tasted the last of her famous beans. I decided to surprise Joe and our sons by adding baked beans to our traditional Christmas dinner.

As I read the recipe for Myrtle's Baked Beans, I realized that, of course, she'd just given me guidelines: my mother had cooked not by recipes, but rather by taste and touch. And I stretched the nonrecipe concept even further. I couldn't find a hambone in our supermarket (I substituted a smoked pork butt) or great northern beans (I substituted navy). The recipe called for soaking the beans overnight. I hadn't found time to do that, but directions on the bean bag indicated I could achieve the same result by simmering them for twenty minutes, then soaking them for an hour.

To coordinate turkey and beans, I decided to cook the beans a day early. While I prepared Christmas Eve dinner, I cooked and tasted the beans. As the afternoon proceeded, I kept adjusting the flavor as my mother always did, adding more brown sugar and molasses. But the beans remained hard and tasteless. I refrigerated them overnight and then the next day gave them as much oven time as I could while I prepared the turkey and stuffing. When I took the bird out to rest, I popped the beans back in. The beans remained crunchy. Nonetheless, I served them. Joe's eyes widened when I brought them to the table.

"You made baked beans!"

They were the first dish he tasted.

After a bite and a short pause, he looked at me and said, "I think you should have baked them a little longer."

I might not have tried to make the beans again, but the following year we bought a Crock-Pot, and I remembered that my sister-in-law Ruth made baked beans in a Crock-Pot, thus leaving her oven free for a large turkey. I called and asked how she cooked her baked beans.

Soak overnight. Simmer for twenty minutes on top of the stove; add the other ingredients; cook in the Crock-Pot on high for an hour, then on low for three more. Ruth asked me what I put in my beans and said she also added ketchup and chopped onions, ingredients not in my mother's recipe. I told her I hadn't been able to find great northerns and had substituted navy beans. That, she said, was the reason my attempt had failed.

A few days later, I received a package from Ruth. In it were packages of great northern beans. Three one-pound bags!

On my second attempt, I sorted the beans (one bag only), soaked them overnight, and simmered them for twenty minutes. I even tested them, sliding the skin off a bean or two to check that they were ready for the next step, as my mother had done. I rinsed them, added new water, and put them back on the stove. Then I added molasses, brown sugar, mustard, and a thick piece of ham, cut into chunks (in lieu of a hambone). I also chopped an onion and added it and the ketchup.

I mixed the ingredients and placed them in the Crock-Pot. All through the afternoon, I interrupted my other tasks to stir and test the beans.

At one point, my son Peter wandered into the kitchen, looked at me stirring the beans yet again, and remarked, "Those beans sure take a lot of cooking."

Later, Stephen walked by just as I was blending a little more molasses into the beans.

"Something smells really good," he said.

"We'll see," I replied.

The beans remained white and crunchy.

In desperation, I turned the Crock-Pot up to high for half an hour, then turned it back to low after adding more molasses, mustard, and brown sugar. Before we left for Midnight Mass, I placed the beans in the refrigerator.

Th next morning, the beans went back into the pot. I stirred and tested and seasoned as I prepared Christmas dinner.

At the table, I carefully watched Joe's expression as he took his first bite. A pause. A smile.

"Ahhh," he said, "there's nothing like baked beans."

The following day, after the excitement of the holiday had been muted—everyone reading gift books or trying out electronic toys—I dished up a portion for myself, poured the remaining Christmas wine into a glass, sat down at the table, and ate the beans, taking time to savor them.

And, yes, those beans *were* good.

AN EARLY RESOLVE

⌐

On each of those trips back to South Dakota and Minnesota, I planned so that I could be at Helen's on a Thursday, the best day for garage sales, and stay through Saturday, the day of the local flea market.

Before I arrived, Helen would pick up the local paper and, by reading descriptions of what was offered, plan an efficient route to the best garage sales. Of course, we both realized that the planning was irrelevant. We'd be lured by signs with arrows pointing this way or that to bargains and, just maybe, undiscovered treasures.

On Thursday and Friday mornings, Helen gave me enough time to drink two cups of coffee while I watched the sunrise paint ever-changing colors on the surface of her lake. But on Saturday morning, she shifted into her standard, "If you want the best, you have to get there first" tempo.

"Barbara! Ready yet? Let's be on our way."

I hastily poured my coffee into a to-go cup and grabbed a straw hat from the coat rack.

"Just pull the door closed behind you," she called, already out in the yard.

I heard a car door slam shut and the motor start up.

It was a short drive, less than five miles, over a gravel road. Down went the windows, up came the country. With lyrics of love and heartbreak as background, we delighted in spotting a whitetail deer and her fawn, and mom and pop ospreys diving for field mice to feed their squalling nestlings. A little farther along, Helen brought her car to an unexpected stop. We watched as a mother skunk, followed by five little ones in a neat line, tails raised high, parade style, crossed the road a few feet in front of us.

The land where the flea market—"swappers' meet," in local parlance—was situated had been a farmer's field. Where once had been wide expanses of soybeans and corn now stood rows and rows of stands and tables. On them were spread out old things of every kind: dishes, tools, machinery parts, furniture. There were new things as well: socks, bedding, towels. Some dealers had placed their things directly on the grass. On and on the displays went.

Helen charged off, but I lagged behind so I could admire a few stands with produce picked just that morning: cabbage, cucumbers, tomatoes, sweet corn, berries of all sorts, even ground cherries that I'd not seen since my childhood, and a riotous display of flowers.

Helen stopped often to speak to people she knew—almost everyone, it seemed. While I examined items that appealed to me, I kept her in my peripheral vision—not an easy task. Conveniently, both of us were interested in the bowls and plates from the 1950s on one table. My eyes were drawn to a large, oval stoneware platter. It was the color and had the smooth texture of river stones.

When she saw my interest, the middle-aged woman standing behind the table spoke up.

"I'll give you a good price on that. It's heavy, and I'm really tired of unpacking it and then having to pack it up all over again at the end of the day."

I ran my hand across its cool surface.

"Oh, it *is* heavy," I said, as I picked it up. "I've never seen anything like this. It's beautiful."

I didn't have to look at Helen to know she was frowning. I was violating a cardinal rule: never show your interest. Doing so signals to the seller that it's time to state a higher-than-usual price.

As I hesitated, the woman asked my name, and, in turn, I asked hers.

"Doris," she told me.

"Well, Barbara," she said, "this really is an unusual piece." And she stated her price.

Helen gave me a sharp nudge. I ignored her and bought it without trying to bargain. "But I don't know how I'll get it home," I said.

"Where's home?" Doris asked, as she began to wrap the platter in old newspapers.

"New York. Manhattan."

"Oh! I grew up in Brooklyn. As a young girl, I spent every summer with my grandparents on their farm in New Jersey. I loved everything about it, especially the animals. I knew when I was very young that one day I'd live on a farm. And that's where I am now."

I laughed. "I grew up on a farm only 120 miles from here. And *I* decided when I was nine, I'd never live on a farm."

"What made you decide that?"

I thought for a moment and recalled the summer I was given the responsibility of planting and tending the garden. I planted rows of peas, green beans, tomatoes, lettuce—the whole works—and, for the first time ever on our farm, green peppers. I hoed, weeded, and watered by dragging that darn hose in and out of the rows. By early July, all the vegetables were thriving, including the pepper plants with their shiny fruit.

"When I stepped out one morning to check on my crop, I was completely unaware of what had happened while I slept. A violent storm had struck in the early-morning hours. All of my plants had been smashed to bits by hail.

"I ran into the kitchen, and as I was telling my mother, my father walked in. The look on his face told us before he even spoke. 'We lost it all. The hail took all of our oats and flax,' he said.

"That morning, I vowed that when I grew up, I'd never, ever be dependent on the weather to earn my living."

"We certainly were determined little gals, weren't we?" Doris said, as she handed the wrapped platter to me.

We looked at each other and nodded. Our smiles a mutual affirmation.

VII. FINALE

FOREIGNER

⌒

If young people knew the future ramifications of the decisions they were about to make, they'd probably freeze and not make any at all. When, as a young woman, I decided to live in New York City, 1,400 miles across the country, I saw it only as a positive. I never considered the drawbacks.

I made that life-altering decision to move to New York a few months after I returned to the United States. I'd been in one of the first groups of Peace Corps volunteers in Thailand, stationed alone in a small town where I was the only Westerner. As the first white person most residents had ever seen, I was a surprising oddity, tall and blond. I stood out in any crowd of locals, who were shorter and darker skinned than I. When I walked through the market, children would cry out, "*Farang! Farang!*" Soon a group would form, all chanting, "Foreigner! Foreigner!" in Thai. I was *always* on show.

When I returned to my home in South Dakota, my hair, bleached from the tropical sun, was the color it had been in my childhood, the same as that of so many others in the community, and no longer was I considered exceptionally tall. Still, I felt off-kilter—adrift and disenfranchised. Questions my family and neighbors asked seemed to broaden the gap between us. The society I'd been a part of in Thailand was so different from theirs that it was difficult to answer the queries without providing extended background synopses. And the ones I did manage to give were woefully inadequate.

For example, there was the Thais' relaxed attitude, and their unwavering reverence for all living creatures. These were at odds with my American "act and solve the problem" mentality. A student, a young girl at the school where I taught, contracted rabies and died. I did everything I could to mitigate the danger of the deadly disease. I managed to convince the principal of the school of the urgency of the situation. She arranged a meeting for me with the governor of the province. After I recited the long and complicated formal phrase to address one of such stature, I explained that the ownerless dogs wandering the streets must be rounded up and killed in order to prevent more deaths. The governor agreed. I was relieved. That is, until I learned that after the dogs were captured, they weren't disposed of, but rather taken a few kilometers away and set free. This made no sense to me, and I had to accept that there was nothing more I could do.

And how could I explain what it was like to be watched, each action of mine noted and remarked upon? So much so that after I shared a bedroom one night, the next morning my roommate announced to everyone present that when I slept, I rolled over in a strange, inefficient manner. Nevertheless, I grew to love my colleagues and to appreciate Thai culture. I was unequipped to explain those conflicting emotions, so I began to withdraw.

I remember with embarrassment how, two days after my return, a local radio show host arranged for a live interview, but when he called at the appointed time, I pretended I was someone else and hung up.

Not all that many years after that decision, those miles became a barrier. At work in Manhattan, I was given only a few days of vacation, my salary was minimal, and plane tickets were expensive. I made that trip only once a year. Years later, I was devastated when I couldn't be with my parents during their medical crises, and I missed my brothers and sisters.

Most painfully, my sons didn't get to know my parents well and didn't receive the special love and attention that only grandparents can give. And Peter and Stephen were never able to visit the farm. The freedom to wander and discover that I enjoyed as a child was never theirs.

Raising two boys in a small Manhattan apartment was a challenge. Peter and Stephen were in school from the late '70s to the early '90s. At that time, even the safest parts of New York City, including the Upper East Side, where we lived, were the scenes of major crimes. Schoolmates were victims of attempted kidnappings. A mother I knew was robbed of her car in midafternoon at gunpoint as she waited to pick up her son from school, the same school that my boys attended. Even when they reached an age where parents in other locales could grant their children freedom, I had to remain ever vigilant.

So when John's wife, Helen, and Bill's wife, Ruth, heard that I was teaching Stephen how to ride a bike in the hallways of our apartment building, they coordinated and issued invitations. Thereafter, Peter and Stephen spent a few weeks each summer in a small town in Indiana and in a suburb of Chicago. There, they ran around outdoors, free from my supervision.

When I had left for Thailand as a young woman, I'd enjoyed the good-spirited commotion of family gatherings, but after my return, I craved time alone. My psyche was trying to reconcile the old me with the new.

When my brothers and their wives came back to the farm to welcome me, I wish I'd acted differently.

After supper one of my brothers said, "Barb, we're about to play a game of cribbage."

Cribbage was traditionally played only by men and boys.

"I'll teach you," Bill offered. "Come join us."

"No, I don't think so. I'm going upstairs to read," I replied.

As a Peace Corps volunteer, I'd been expected to be an exemplar of American culture, while at the same time fitting seamlessly into the life of my village, which was still firmly bound by old mores. Back at home, I felt the constrictions of small-town life with a new awareness. I couldn't imagine staying, living under ever-vigilant eyes.

I was eager to pursue my career as a newspaper reporter. New York City seemed the perfect place to do that. New York City was all about writing and authors, art and music! It was an easy decision.

CRIBBAGE

M y brothers still play cribbage. The rhythm of their words as they tally up their hands, and the satisfaction apparent in the winner's voice, still echo in my subconscious. "Fifteen/two, fifteen/four, and a pair is six."

At home, my father and brothers played cribbage as competitively as the men in town. Pauses of concentration were short-lived, interrupted often by shouts of jubilation as the final score was called out. No prizes were given. However, after John and Bill left for college, my father and Bob agreed upon a reward for the winner of two out of three hands. The loser of the two had to head out to the barn alone to milk the cows. The winner's award was to stay in the house and enjoy a second cup of coffee.

ROOTS AND LEAVES

⟋

None of Roy and Myrtle's children remained in South Dakota. All of us moved to other states to pursue our careers. But as my siblings established their lives in places far from the farm, they found ways to stay connected to their origins.

John, who as a child maintained a tiny plot of corn behind the lilac bushes, earned his PhD in agronomy and became renowned as a breeder of hybrid corn. He worked and raised his family in Indiana. Now retired, he continues a pet research project. Each January, he germinates mung bean seeds by placing them in pots in a bedroom window where they mature. Then he plants that new generation of seeds in a field.

Throughout the summer he weeds and tends the plants, and in the fall he selects the best of that new bean crop. And so the cycle continues. This involves hard physical labor. His goal is to develop a mung bean hybrid that can be sown into growing wheat fields in order to produce an additional crop of grain from the same acreage each year. Successfully developing his hybrid would mean more grain to feed the burgeoning population worldwide. As this book goes to press, he'll be celebrating his eighty-sixth birthday by harvesting his latest crop.

Bill raised his family in a suburb of Chicago, where he oversaw a lab devoted to maintaining safety and increasing cheese production for Kraft. After retiring from that job, he became a realtor and established a home property management company.

One of the houses that he maintained was located near the Des Plaines River, and, just as Bill had struggled to keep the Whetstone River's water from flooding our childhood home, he found himself sandbagging once again when that river flooded. Twice he was successful, once he was not, and the house went underwater. Concurrent with that business enterprise, for twenty years he worked with the homeless by helping provide shelter and maintaining the houses.

He began accumulating houses as a sideline. Gardens, also. Over the years, he's experimented with new varieties of vegetables and fruit. Some of those have failed, others have been a success—so much so that now he is a benevolent greengrocer to neighbors and friends, giving away quarts of berries and bushels of vegetables each year. He keeps a log fastened to the back of a cupboard door where he notes the quantities he's handed out to the lucky folks. His tomatoes are especially prized; I try to time my annual visit to coincide with the peak of his tomato harvest.

As Bob has moved from state to state, he's always held jobs related to agriculture. His latest, in North Dakota, involves advising individual soybean and corn farmers. After he tests the soil of their fields, he informs them of the correct ratio of nutrients to use in order to produce maximum crop yields. He does this during North Dakota's short growing season.

At age sixty-five, Bob began this annual routine: After the field work is done in November, he drives south to a location in the mountains of Texas along the banks of the Rio Grande. There, he works alone as a predator controller, trapping bobcats and mountain lions. Alone? Yes, alone, despite the fact that all of us remind him that doing so is not wise for a man over eighty. Occasionally, his day is interrupted when he rescues struggling migrants from Mexico whom human smugglers, known as coyotes, have abandoned in that harsh environment.

In the months following Hurricane Katrina, the three brothers banded together and, harnessing their singular, independent personalities, drove to Mississippi, where they helped rebuild houses ravaged by that historic storm.

Helen has always lived near Minneapolis, where she worked as a secretary. Later, she began her antique business. Each year, at every house she's lived in, she's planted both a vegetable and a fruit garden, until the latest house, whose location in a more remote area with an abundant deer and raccoon population makes raising vegetables impossible, but, as always, she tends an abundant, colorful flower garden.

Easy access to fishing has compensated for the lost satisfaction of growing her own vegetables. Just as she had to walk only a short way from our house to toss a line from her spot on the Big Rock into our river, she has only to walk a few yards from her latest house down to a lake, where she fishes from her dock.

Patt, who was a high school teacher and librarian in the St. Louis area, always bought homes with enough acreage to allow for—true to her personality—very well-tended gardens. After she retired, she bought farmland outside the small town where she lived. She rented that acreage to farmers, who grew corn and soybeans. Black walnut trees grew on a hilly portion of that farm. In the fall, she gathered the fallen nuts from those trees. She gave away some and used the others in her baking. I remember nibbling her delicious walnut cookies as we played Scrabble.

At one point, when she was forced to live in a small apartment for a short time, she said (and we thought) she'd go crazy. She couldn't survive without grass and flowers and the natural world.

My love of nature is at my core, too. I always take notice of flowers and trees before man-made structures. This was true as my childhood urge to see the world drove me the farthest of our clan—to Thailand—where I taught as a Peace Corps volunteer. And beyond. During breaks in the school schedule, I visited Hong Kong, Cambodia, and the Philippines. And then, on an exhilarating trip home to the United States with Georgia, my friend and fellow adventurer, the two of us maximized our return tickets to see as much as we could. As long as we were heading west toward the United States, our tickets allowed us to make as many stops as we wished.

As two young women traveling alone at that time (the early '60s), we stood out and were assumed to have money. We might have been robbed or worse.

From Bangkok we flew to Rangoon (now Yangon). At that time, an oppressive military dictatorship controlled Burma (Myanmar). At the airport security checkpoint, heavily armed guards detained us, pulling us aside and into a small room. The portable typewriter I carried made us suspect. They examined it using flashlights, making sure we hadn't hidden any contraband in the innards of its mechanism. The security officials were convinced we were CIA operatives or, almost as bad, journalists. Finally we were cleared but allowed to stay only one night. Georgia and I hurried to see as much of the city as we could.

Then we flew to India, Nepal (its borders had been opened to tourists only a decade before), Iran, and on to Lebanon. At that time, its capital, Beirut, was called the Paris of the Middle East. Georgia and I fell in love with the city and found reasons to keep postponing our departure. We managed to find an apartment, and, remarkably, we each found a job. We lived there for six months. After Georgia left to return to the United States, I made a side trip to Jerusalem, which was then still within the borders of Jordan. Wanting to see more, but with my funds near zero, I made one last stop—in Greece.

Through all those countries, I took special note of the flowers and trees. I wish there'd been a way to capture and retain the fragrances—the heady, sweet scent of Thailand's jasmine; the delicate aroma of Burma's orchids; the spicy smell of the ancient cedar trees on the slopes of Lebanon's mountains—so I could breathe them in one more time and, in so doing, reinvigorate my memories.

A few months after I moved to New York, Joe and I reconnected. Joe was also from Big Stone City. We'd actually gone to the same church and attended the same high school, but we hadn't paid much attention to each other at the time. After all, I was a senior and he was only a junior.

In New York City, our mutual love of the visual arts, American history, hiking, and classical music was a magnet that drew us together. We dated for two years and then married in 1968. Whenever our work schedules allowed, we traveled, in the United States and Canada and throughout Europe. As years went by and we welcomed Peter and Stephen into our lives, we took them with us whenever possible.

Sadly, although Patt was the one who fueled my wanderlust with her fabulous tales of Arabia, Alaska, and Latin America, she never was able to explore as she had once dreamed, but she always listened intently as I told stories of my adventures.

Dorothy, of course, never traveled. She's buried in the Catholic cemetery, a mile from where she was born and a mile from our farmhouse, where she spent her life.

MASS OF THE ANGELS

〰

Through the years, when I've pondered Dorothy's place in our family's world, I've always begun with the assumption that her birth was an unmitigated catastrophe, a tragedy. Now, after doing some research, I'm not so sure.

During the last decades of the nineteenth and the first decades of the twentieth centuries, infant and maternal death rates were high in rural areas of our region. Even when mother and baby survived childbirth, each was susceptible to infectious diseases that were often deadly. There was a paucity of doctors, insufficient—and often incorrect—medical knowledge, and an inability to provide sanitary conditions. And, perhaps most important, before the discovery of penicillin in 1928, no antibiotics existed.

My mother's mother and baby brother both died from typhoid fever. My mother, her sister Marian, and their brother, Brit, were hospitalized but survived that same epidemic. Mother was so weakened by the disease that months later the doctor advised that she delay enrolling in elementary school. Therefore, she and Marian, who was ten months younger, were in the same grade and graduated from high school the same year.

In light of the time, 1927, and place, rural Minnesota, Dorothy's birth may have been viewed as a partial success. Mother and baby did survive.

When we celebrated my son's first birthday, I called my mother from Manhattan. I didn't need to remind her of the importance of the day. She beat me to it.

"Congratulations!" Her voice was warm and strong. "Peter is one year old today! Reaching one is such an important milestone!"

In the 1920s, one in ten babies did not live to see their first year. Mother never took for granted that a baby would survive, be healthy, and live a full year.

As a mother of seven, she must have felt as if she was always nursing at least one sick child. As there were no vaccinations for some childhood diseases yet, schools served as efficient incubators for illness.

A year after I graduated from college, I visited my parents on the farm. None of my siblings were there. With my parents napping and no one to distract me, I left the house. A walk was my established routine.

It was mid-March. Spring was a long way off.

I've always appreciated the preludes to spring and fall as much as—maybe more than—the full-blown versions: the first hint of spring to come forecast by a few shoots of grass or small buds emerging on a willow; the glories of impending fall found in the yellowing of the leaves on an oak or the swelling of a seedpod on a milkweed plant.

In some parts of China, the people recognize these "between times" by dividing the solar calendar into twenty-four seasons, naming them with lyrical aptness—for example, "awakening of the insects" and "frost descends."

On that solitary venture, I didn't go into the woods, as usual, but instead walked up the drive, turned left at the cottonwood tree, and began to climb the hill. Partway up the slope, I stepped off the drive and onto a field. Too small and rocky to till and plant, it remained virgin prairie. A few patches of snow dotted the hill. I hoped to find a chink in nature's winter armor, in the form of an early pasque blossom. In our area it's called mayflower, a misnomer because it usually blooms well before the beginning of May.

When I was a child, my mother and I would search here, scanning the dull brown grass for this harbinger of spring. It's not the same pasque blossom you'll find in gardens today throughout the temperate zone. Those flowers are hybrids—bred to be tall and showy. The one I was looking for is short and doesn't draw attention to itself. A person must have a sharp eye to spy it.

Even before the first blade of fresh green grass pops up from newly unfrozen fields, the pale lavender flower, not bothering to wait for its leaves to sprout, pushes up as a bud. Then, as sun warms it, the blossom opens to reveal an orange center. When a breeze blows, it wavers on its soft stem.

There was no sign of any blossom, so I crossed over the neighbors' driveway and kept walking northward to an area where I'd never been. A bramble of wild raspberries, composed of interlocking, winding stems covered with sharp thorns, formed a barrier ahead of me. If it had been summer, I never would have tried working my way through the dense growth, but because there were no leaves on the vines, I could see a narrow opening. Probably a deer path, I thought, and slowly forged ahead.

Sloping down to a thicket of trees was another small piece of virgin prairie. I stopped and looked ahead. I blinked to clear my vision. There, just before the tree line, I saw two small shapes, both the same color as the dead grass surrounding them. When I walked closer, I was shocked to see that they were gravestones. They'd been carved from some kind of soft stone that had suffered from the extreme temperatures. I was shaken by this unexpected reminder of death. The headstones were misshapen, and lichen had drawn crude patches of orange on their surfaces. A recumbent baby lamb carved from the same kind of stone rested atop each one. Feeling as though I were desecrating a sacred spot, I hesitated and then slowly walked closer in order to read the inscriptions, but neither names nor dates were legible.

These graves had been forgotten for decades. The land belonged to my father's cousin, who lived at the foot of this hill. That man had inherited the farm from his father. The children—I assumed they were children because of the lambs—had not been members of that branch of our family, nor were they any of our relatives, all of whom are buried in town cemeteries. I felt unmoored by this discovery of a family's grief and mourned for the two young ones buried here. I turned, walked back up the hill, and headed home.

In the year 2000, each of my siblings and I traveled long distances to Pierre, South Dakota, for the internment of my mother's youngest sister, Mabel—the last of that generation. After the short ceremony in the Catholic cemetery, we paid our respects to our ancestors—my mother's parents and her four grandparents are all buried there. Then we separated and wandered.

I looked toward the north. There, at a distance from the main cluster of graves, was a row of tombstones. Each was small, some more elaborate than others. When I read the inscriptions, I realized all of the stones marked children's graves. Why were these little ones not buried with their families? Why were they not in the family plots behind me? I felt a deep sorrow grip me, stronger than the one I'd felt earlier at my aunt's grave site, for she had lived well into her nineties.

There was a caretaker talking to a small group. I waited until he was free and then approached him.

"Excuse me, can you tell me why the children are buried in that row at the edge of the cemetery?" I asked him, pointing to the line of miniature tombstones.

"Oh, that's the Wall of Tears."

"Wall of Tears? What do you mean?"

"In the old days, people didn't know much about how diseases were spread. There were terrible epidemics in those times. Folks thought the bodies of the little ones could pass infection on to visitors."

Then, probably sensing my anguish, he added, "I can assure you we tend those graves just as well as we do the others."

I thanked him, turned away from all the gravestones, and slowly walked to the western edge of the cemetery. The Missouri River meandered a short distance away, and above it, in great hillocks, rose the bluffs. Looking at them, I remembered how my mother had spoken wistfully of the Missouri River Bluffs. She, her sisters, and their friends had wandered these cliffs every spring, searching for that first blossom of the season— the pasque flower.

And then, when I looked toward the small headstones, I remembered how, when I was about the same age Dorothy had been when she died, Mother told me about Dorothy's funeral. Father Esterguard had decided to say a Mass of the Angels and so had donned white, not black, vestments. After the funeral, he explained to my mother why he had done that.

"It was the appropriate thing to do. Dorothy never sinned. She was as pure as an angel."

As my mother told me about this, I saw her shoulders relax and heard her voice soften.

NO RECORD

⌐

It was at that stage of development when a young person is convinced she knows more than her parents that I returned to visit my mother and father in 1974. By that time, they had sold the farm and moved into a small trailer home at the edge of Big Stone City. Each of them was struggling with serious health issues. My mother had already made painful decisions about what possessions to sell or give away when they'd moved from the farmhouse, but now, knowing that a move to a nursing home was in the near future, she was whittling down her things even more, to just the bare necessities.

One day my mother said, "Would you sort the photographs, Barbara? Take yours, and put the rest in envelopes for the others."

So that evening, after we'd eaten, washed the dishes, and gotten my baby son settled for at least part of the night, I opened the cedar chest and lifted out a large, lovely coat box, saved from some long-ago purchase. The chest had been part of my mother's trousseau and had always sat in the dining room of our farmhouse. It served as the storage unit for photographs and small keepsakes. It was one of the few pieces of furniture that had made the cut to be saved and had been moved to the trailer home.

Viewing decades-old pictures is always difficult. The task was made harder for me because I'd always regretted—actually resented—that no one had cared enough to have a professional portrait taken of me, alone or with my siblings. There were only two snapshots from before I entered school. In each, I'm about a year old and sitting on our lawn. In one, my baby face is squinting against the bright sun; in the other, I appear more comfortable, but that photo is crinkled at the edges. I'm told that a snapshot of me—or more than one—was taken at the birthday party Helen gave me when I turned six, but the only ones that survive from that day are of my friends, guests at the party. There aren't any of me.

I found the process of looking at the photographs very unsettling. An hour earlier, I'd been dining with my aging parents; the next, I was looking at photos of them as young adults.

I sorted and made stacks for my siblings and me. In the box were beautiful engagement portraits of my mother and father; their wedding picture, which, even though it was taken in the backyard of my mother's childhood home, was the work of a professional photographer; the timeless one of my siblings taken in a photographer's studio in Ortonville; and each of our graduation portraits. I was startled anew when I discovered the snapshot of Dorothy. I'd seen it once before, when I was a teenager and digging through the photo box. She was lying in a wicker carriage, her head covered by a bonnet.

I ponder what I did next. Given my unending disappointment that there was no photograph taken of my younger self with my siblings, how could I have done what I did? After I gathered mine together—the squinting one, the wrinkled one, my graduation photos—I didn't hesitate to add the snapshot of Dorothy to my stack. If my mother saw it, her grief would be renewed. That was my thinking. I now realize that wasn't my decision to make. Perhaps my mother would have found comfort in holding that photo, at seeing Dorothy's face again.

Shortly after that visit, I made an appointment with the finest children's photographer in Manhattan to capture Peter's likeness at six months. I did the same when our second son, Stephen, was a baby, making sure that his portrait was taken at the same age. I wasn't going to let either of my children ever have reason to feel as if he hadn't been valued as an infant, that he had been loved less than the other.

Now, of course, the photographer was in business. So each of these sessions evolved into many poses of the baby, followed by many poses of mother and baby. Today, in the bottom of my cedar chest (no, sadly, not my mother's) is a large, flat box that protects those beautiful portraits of my sons. Both would be mortified if I put them on display now.

On the last visit to the photographer's studio, Joe joined us and a family portrait was taken. In that photo, Peter is a permanent age six, Stephen a permanent age three. And that portrait of the four of us has a permanent place on the piano.

In 2017, knowing my family had only memories and a snapshot to document Dorothy's life—and with my sense of guilt at having taken the photo driving me—I decided to obtain a copy of her birth certificate. I phoned the courthouse in Ortonville, the location of the births of all my parents' children, and asked to speak to the register of deeds. I was transferred to Eileen. I explained to her what I was looking for.

"Yes, I can help you," she said. "How do you spell that name? And what year would that be?"

I spelled the name and told her 1927.

"No, that name's not here. Let me go back a year."

"That's not necessary," I said. "I'm sure of the year. All of us were born in Ortonville. And I know my birth certificate is there, because I've requested and received copies of it."

"Well, just let me go ahead anyway and see what we have. Oh, here's Helen, 1929, and Patricia, 1930 . . . ," and she continued on to me, the last.

"Thank you very much. I appreciate your help," I said, and hung up the phone.

There was no birth certificate for Dorothy? I was disappointed and perplexed. The next morning, the reason came to me. There was no birth certificate because Dorothy wasn't expected to live, so the doctor didn't report her birth to the county.

There's only a small granite stone, a single photo, and these words I write to mark her life.

DIRT, REVISITED

‿⟶

As I reread what I've written, I see that on a shelf above my desk there's a book entitled *Dirt*. I'm grateful it survived the move from our country house; so many of my books did not. I take it down, and a sheet of yellowed paper floats out. I unfold it and read these notes I scribbled years ago.

> *Cleaning dirt from under my fingernails*
> *before dressing for the prom*
> *Mud oozing between our toes wading in the river*
> *Dirt in the creases of my father's forehead*
> *Mud, sucking strong, impossible to drive through*
> *Moist dirt mounded above my mother's grave*
> *Dirt frozen too hard to take my father's coffin*
> *Dirt*
> *Damned dirt*
> *Blessed dirt*

RETURNING HOME

T his was the first trip back since my father's funeral. I thought it would be truly depressing, but it was so wonderful having us all together, the knowledge that neither our mother nor our father would be there didn't really hit hard. Until, that is, everyone decided to drive down and look at our farm.

We jammed ourselves into one car. When we turned off the highway, I was vaguely aware that the dirt road had been widened and its surface topped with gravel. Different, altered, changed. I should have begun to prepare myself for what I'd see at the end of that road. My brothers were loudly but good-naturedly arguing about some detail of the past, so no one heard my moan of pain. Even though I'd visited a few times after the barn had burned while my parents still lived there, it was a horrible shock as we turned the corner at the bottom of the hill to see a one-story concrete building where the tall barn had once stood. During all those years, the traditional wooden structure and its companion silo had continued to reside in my mind. The fire had not deleted its image.

Of course, I knew that another family—a nonfarming family—now owned our place, but again I wasn't prepared for what I saw as we continued. The house, even though I knew it had long been painted brown, shook me. I looked away.

The curves and twists of the river had changed also, but that didn't upset me. Floods had been causing that to happen forever.

My brothers were busy commenting on the improvements the new owners had made. I was trying not to notice those changes. But I couldn't help but see the awful gap where the lilac bushes on the south side of our lawn once bloomed. All of them—purple, lavender, white—had been pulled out. Worse, the wildflowers that Patt had dug from the woods and planted by the kitchen door, and that my mother had faithfully watered for years, were no more.

And there was no way I could ignore what was happening to the beautiful old cottonwood. A part of our day-to-day childhood was dying. We always made that tree the goal of our races: "I'll race you to the cottonwood and back." Now, its beautiful crown showed gaps and there was an ugly crack in its huge trunk. A metal band encircled its circumference—an effort, I assumed, to hold it together.

But it was only when we began to drive back to town that I became aware of the worst sacrilege. The new owners had lowered the hill. Cutting down? Filling in? I don't know how they did it, but now the big hill was only a slope. It seemed as though I was the only one of my siblings who was upset.

When I voiced my indignation, Bob didn't miss a beat. "Just goes to show that you're older than the hills," he told me.

Our hill had offered challenges—for fun and for survival. When winter set in and there was a good covering of snow, we'd carry the long sled to the top of the hill. If he were there, John, my oldest brother, would climb on first. No matter the makeup of the group, the oldest got the premier spot. In descending order of size, the others would climb on, one on top of the other. Saying a prayer that we wouldn't hit the cottonwood, the last would make a run for it and, at the final moment, slam on. Off we'd speed. The top person would fall off, sooner or later. Then another and another would topple down. Often the only one who arrived at our front door still on the sled was the lucky rider on the bottom. This enterprise was the biggest challenge at night when there was no moon, only stars, to give us light.

That was all about fun. There was no inkling of that fun when we drove up the hill when it was covered in mud or snow or, worst of all, coated with ice. That sharp curve, just before the steep incline, made it essential that the driver hit the gas pedal with just enough force at just the right location to give the car enough momentum to make it to the top—without sliding off into the ditch. If we didn't make it to the top, the only option was to back down the treacherous surface and start all over. No wonder Mother's reaction as we climbed into the car was always the same: "Let's say a Hail Mary."

Our farm is gone. What I loved is no more.

When I'm dying—if I'm given half an hour's notice—I'll drive that bumpy old road one more time. When I start out, I'll take those winding curves slowly, roll down the window and smell the sweet clover and wild roses of summer. Or perhaps I'll make it early spring and stop the car when I'm almost there. Walk on the small field of virgin prairie again. Maybe I'll be lucky and find the first flower of spring, the delicate, pale lavender pasque, with its fuzzy little stem. Stop to listen to the birds. I'll climb back in, and as I approach the hill—the hill the way it should be—I'll speed up, take that curve a little too fast so that the car rocks a bit, and then . . .

There it will be, the way it once was! The cottonwood green and healthy; the barn tall and strong; and the house white—oh, yes, white again! And, of course, the river beyond.

ACKNOWLEDGMENTS

With gratitude, I'd like to acknowledge the following:

First and foremost, my two sons, Peter and Stephen, for their advice and support throughout, even before, this memoir was begun.

My siblings, Helen Allen, John Hoffbeck, Bill Hoffbeck, and Bob Hoffbeck, who remembered with me and who never doubted that I would—someday—get this done. And to my dear departed sister, Patt Johnson, who always encouraged me to write.

My teachers, all of whom were generous with their advice and time: Barbara Ascher, Walter Bode, Lan Samantha Chang, Ellen Feldman, Daphne Merkin, Marion Roach Smith, and Meg Wolitzer.

Lewis Burke Frumkes, who through his writing programs and his enthusiasm for all things word related made it possible for me to study with outstanding authors.

My friends and supportive critics, Bridgette Devine, Mary Drayne, Don Haight, Vicky Myers, Diana Nash, Helen Pomeroy, Ruth Sussman, Josie Vania, and Colleen Wahl, and my dear departed friend and fellow adventurer, Georgia Kirillin Han, who urged me to "get going" with this so many years ago.

My editor, Annie Tucker, who helped shape these pieces into a meaningful whole; my loyal and tireless assistant, Mariah Plante; and Jack Hamelburg, who in his illustrations captured the images in my head.

The New York Society Library, especially its head librarian, Carolyn Waters, and the members of my memoir-writing group.

To all, my deepest thanks.

Gathering details for this book was similar to trying to capture shifting streams in a current of water. Often, the details of these family stories were hard to pin down. Events changed my parents' temperaments, so the father my older siblings knew was not the same man I grew up with. And he treated his sons very differently than he did his daughters. And, of course, the ages and the personalities of us children kept shifting, as is true of all families. None of us remembers the same incident in exactly the same way.

Bob, who lives in North Dakota for half the year and in Texas for the other six months, became a willing coresearcher. He traveled to Pierre to read the names and dates on family tombstones, and, a year later, to the Grant County courthouse to verify the date my grandfather had purchased our house. On that visit, the assistant register of deeds spent over an hour helping him locate relevant papers. She told Bob that our house was on the move! Plans had been made for it to be loaded onto a flatbed truck and hauled to another location on our former property, to a place I know well. It will be placed on the banks of the Whetstone River, not far from where I found the buttercups in "The Flood."

How did she know that the building was about to be moved? Because she'd been raised in that very same house.

When, at last, I had the opportunity to devote whole days to writing and researching for this book, I began to wake in the middle of the night with a phrase, a better word, the proper placement of a particular story. I began to keep paper and pen on my nightstand. When inspiration hit, I'd turn on the lamp and jot down a few words. In the morning, I'd make sense of my scribbles and, often, take advantage of those notes. My brain was working while I slept.

I woke very early one morning with a terrible sense of fear. Half-awake, I was back in the kitchen of our farmhouse. Mother and I were alone. We had heard a terrible cry, which had been followed by crashing and bellowing. I bounded down the steps from my bedroom, meeting my mother just as she dashed into the kitchen.

"It's a cougar!" she yelled, as she grabbed a shotgun and ran outside.

I was frantic. "Don't go! Don't go!" My chest tightened.

Now fully awake, I stood alone in my bedroom in New York City.

That was all I remembered of that night. It was so vivid. I waited until it was a reasonable hour and then called my brother Bob.

"Do you think that really happened? Why were Mother and I alone?"

"Oh, yes," Bob said. "That happened, all right. A cougar attacked our cows directly below the house. They stampeded, broke through fences that had never been broken before. The cougar slashed one cow down her withers. Years later, when you touched that scarred area, she still shuddered with pain. It took us two days to round up all the cows. But you and Mother weren't alone that night. It was well past midnight. We were all in bed. Dad and I had to pull on some clothes. We were there in less than a minute."

In my quest, I've asked questions, listened, and taken notes; returned and researched; dreamed and remembered. And now, at last, the stories are written.

Hoffbeck farmstead; summer 1927. Photo taken by Mabel Chaussee.

Roy and Myrtle on their wedding day. September 9, 1926.

Dorothy, 1928

(Standing) Patt, age seven; Helen, age eight.
(Sitting) John, age five; Bill, age three. 1937

Barbara, about one-year-old

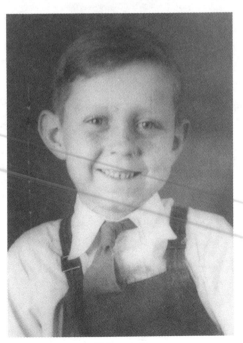

Bob, age six

Barbara, age nine

Bob, Barbara, John, Bill with giant cucumber. c. 1947

Remnants of a flood. Year unknown

*Barbara saying goodbye to students and fellow teachers
at the airport in Bangkok, Thailand 1965*

Peter, Joe, Barbara, Stephen 1981

Barbara sitting on the Big Rock on the bank of the Whetstone River.
October 1989

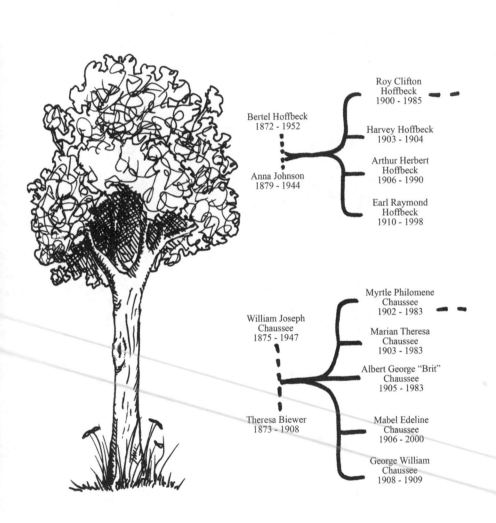

Bertel Hoffbeck
1872 - 1952

Anna Johnson
1879 - 1944

Roy Clifton
Hoffbeck
1900 - 1985

Harvey Hoffbeck
1903 - 1904

Arthur Herbert
Hoffbeck
1906 - 1990

Earl Raymond
Hoffbeck
1910 - 1998

William Joseph
Chaussee
1875 - 1947

Theresa Biewer
1873 - 1908

Myrtle Philomene
Chaussee
1902 - 1983

Marian Theresa
Chaussee
1903 - 1983

Albert George "Brit"
Chaussee
1905 - 1983

Mabel Edeline
Chaussee
1906 - 2000

George William
Chaussee
1908 - 1909

This family tree has had to be truncated in the interest of clarity and conserving space. As a result, many beloved sisters-in-law, cousins, nieces, and nephews have been excluded. I hope this book will encourage the younger generations to write the next chapter of our family's history.

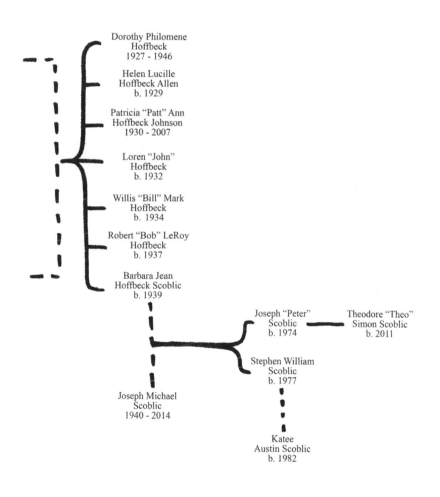

Dorothy Philomene
Hoffbeck
1927 - 1946

Helen Lucille
Hoffbeck Allen
b. 1929

Patricia "Patt" Ann
Hoffbeck Johnson
1930 - 2007

Loren "John"
Hoffbeck
b. 1932

Willis "Bill" Mark
Hoffbeck
b. 1934

Robert "Bob" LeRoy
Hoffbeck
b. 1937

Barbara Jean
Hoffbeck Scoblic
b. 1939

Joseph "Peter"
Scoblic
b. 1974

Theodore "Theo"
Simon Scoblic
b. 2011

Stephen William
Scoblic
b. 1977

Joseph Michael
Scoblic
1940 - 2014

Katee
Austin Scoblic
b. 1982

ABOUT THE AUTHOR

Barbara Hoffbeck Scoblic's writing career began as a reporter for the Sioux Falls (South Dakota) Argus Leader, and continued in New York City at G.P. Putnam's Sons. She now lives and writes in New York City.

Author photo ©: Nina Subin Photography

Selected Titles From She Writes Press

She Writes Press is an independent publishing company founded to serve women writers everywhere. Visit us at www.shewritespress.com.

The Beauty of What Remains: Family Lost, Family Found by Susan Johnson Hadler. $16.95, 978-1-63152-007-5. Susan Johnson Hadler goes on a quest to find out who the missing people in her family were—and what happened to them—and succeeds in reuniting a family shattered for four generations.

The Coconut Latitudes: Secrets, Storms, and Survival in the Caribbean by Rita Gardner. $16.95, 978-1-63152-901-6. A haunting, lyrical memoir about a dysfunctional family's experiences in a reality far from the envisioned Eden—and the terrible cost of keeping secrets.

All the Ghosts Dance Free: A Memoir by Terry Cameron Baldwin. $16.95, 978-1-63152-822-4. A poetic memoir that explores the legacy of alcoholism and teen suicide in one woman's life—and her efforts to create an authentic existence in the face of that legacy.

The Butterfly Groove: A Mother's Mystery, A Daughter's Journey by Jessica Barraco. $16.95, 978-1-63152-800-2. In an attempt to solve the mystery of her deceased mother's life, Jessica Barraco retraces the older woman's steps nearly forty years earlier—and finds herself along the way.

The S Word by Paolina Milana. $16.95, 978-1-63152-927-6. An insider's account of growing up with a schizophrenic mother, and the disastrous toll the illness—and her Sicilian Catholic family's code of secrecy—takes upon her young life.

The Sportscaster's Daughter: A Memoir by Cindi Michael. $16.95, 978-1-63152-107-2. Despite being disowned by her father—sportscaster George Michael, said to be the man who inspired ESPN's *SportsCenter*—Cindi Michael manages financially and heals emotionally, ultimately finding confidence from within.